# Nyanga Flowers

# Nyanga Flowers

by

## Mary Clarke

BAOBAB BOOKS

Publication of *Nyanga Flowers* has been made possible by generous donations granted by the following organizations:

AFRICAN DISTILLERS LIMITED

aac ANGLO AMERICAN CORPORATION ZIMBABWE LIMITED

Additional funding is acknowledged from: Beverley Building Society, Central African Cables Ltd, First Merchant Bank of Central Africa Ltd, Gulliver Consolidated Ltd, Mashonaland Holdings Ltd, National Foods Ltd, Rennie Grinaker Zimbabwe Ltd and Zimleaf Holdings (Pvt.) Ltd.

The author and publishers record their appreciation to all organizations that made possible this unique venture in Zimbabwean book publishing.

First published in 1991 by
BAOBAB BOOKS, a division of Academic Books (Pvt.) Ltd.
P.O. Box 567, Harare, Zimbabwe

Copyright © *Illustrations & Text:* Mary Clarke

*Book Design & Production:* Bruce Brine
*Map by:* Lorraine Mons
*Typesetting on Apple Computers:* Academic Books (Pvt.) Ltd.
*Filmsetting:* Waughco (Pvt.) Ltd., Harare
*Colour Separations:* Colorscan (Pvt.) Ltd., Harare
*Origination:* Haylett-Litho (Pvt.) Ltd., Harare
*Printed by:* National Printing & Packaging (Pvt.) Ltd., Harare
*Bound by:* Bremner Bookbinders, Greendale, Harare

ISBN 0 908 311 34 6
ISBN 0 908 311 37 0 (Limited edition)

# Contents

page

About this book .......................................... 7

Map of the Nyanga area .............................. 8

Setting the scene .......................................... 9

JANUARY – in the wet ................................ 21

FEBRUARY – orchids in bloom .................. 39

MARCH – the purple hills ............................ 55

APRIL – the everlasting flowers .................. 73

MAY – looking at ferns ................................ 85

JUNE – aloes ablaze .................................... 95

JULY – burning of firebreaks ...................... 105

AUGUST – musasa time ................................ 115

SEPTEMBER – the phoenix flowers ............ 125

OCTOBER – sunshine .................................. 141

NOVEMBER– the start of the rains ............ 155

DECEMBER – a month of storms ................ 165

Bibliography and suggested reading .............. 177

Index to family names and groups ................ 179

Index to plants illustrated and common names ................ 183

6  NYANGA FLOWERS

# About this book

As a geographer writing a book about plants, it is not surprising that my notes and pictures have ended up more environmental than botanical.

With no scientific background my approach has been that of a nature lover finding out about the flowers around me. It has been a voyage of discovery as exciting as any venture into the unknown.

Bob Drummond of the National Herbarium in Harare agreed to look at the drawings and paintings and to help with the identification. Without him this book would not have been possible. He has been very patient, spending long hours helping, yet not attempting to influence my style which must often have made him wince.

I would also like to thank Bud Payne of the Nyanga Experiment Station for helping me set the scene. His knowledge and love of the area made me realize that he, not I, should have written this introduction.

Nyanga has a wealth of plant material: I have found 96 species of ferns alone, most of them within walking distance of my home at 'Blue Mountains'.

No one book could cover more than a subjective selection. If what you are looking for is not illustrated perhaps another of the family is. The family index on page 179 may help.

Throughout the book, scientific names have been used. Where a common name is in general use and where I have been able to find a Chimanica name they have been included in either the text or in the index, but no attempt has been made to invent names. Botanical names are often a mixture of Latin and Greek, or with place or people's names with Latin endings. However, they are mostly descriptive and therefore helpful. Plants are divided into orders, classes and families. The families are then divided into genera, and it is this generic name that comes first in the text, followed by the specific name of the species. Sometimes there are subspecies and sometimes variations to further subdivide the species.

Please remember that many plants have extended flowering periods and that climatic factors may delay or advance flowering.

Although this is a book on Nyanga, most of the plants illustrated occur elsewhere in the Eastern Highlands and many are found throughout the highveld of Zimbabwe.

Mary Clarke
Nyanga 1991

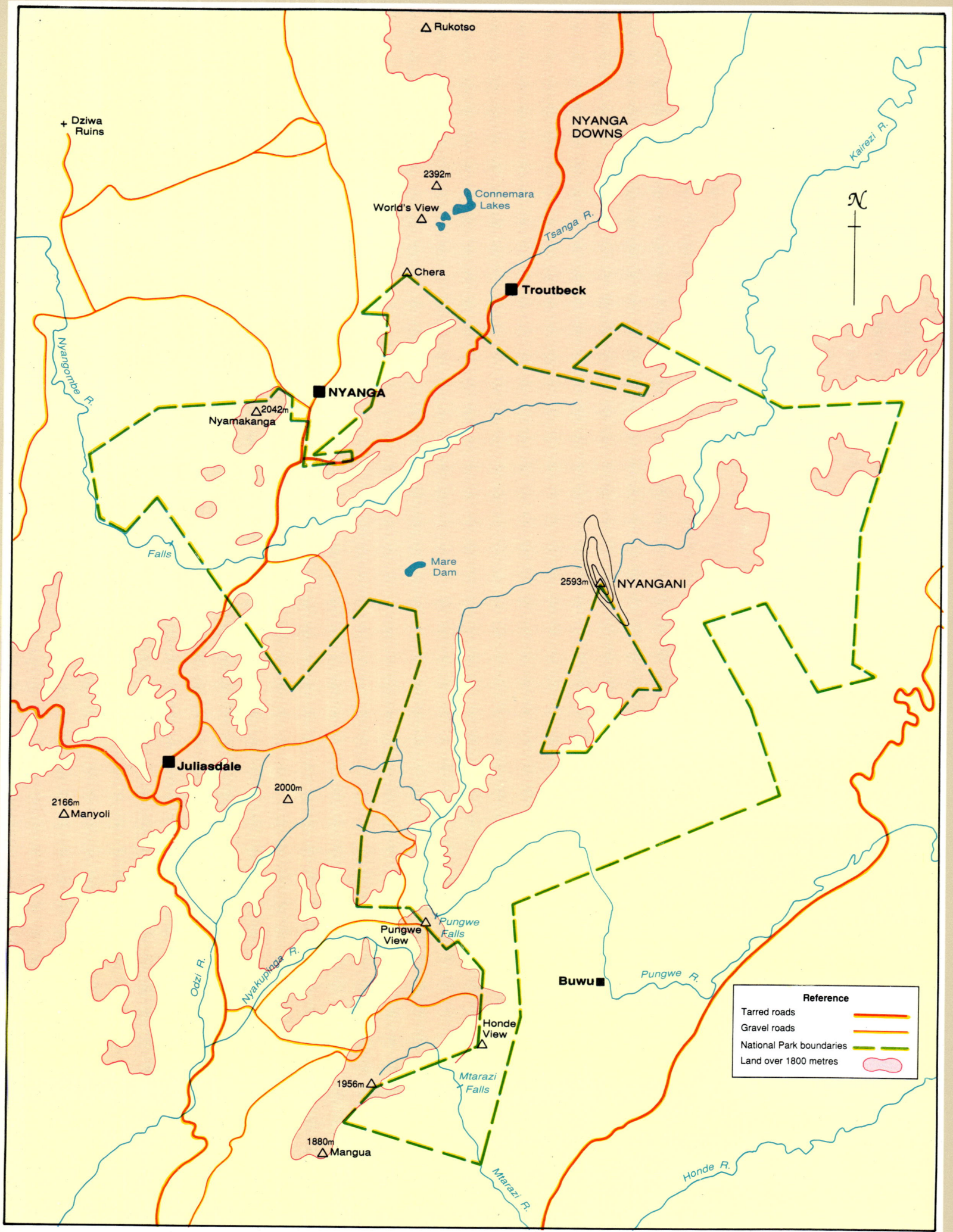

Reference
Tarred roads
Gravel roads
National Park boundaries
Land over 1800 metres

NYANGA
DOWNS

Rukotso

2392m
World's View
Connemara Lakes

Chera
Troutbeck

Tsanga R.

Kairezi R.

Dziwa Ruins

Nyangombe R.

NYANGA
2042m
Nyamakanga

Falls

Mare Dam

2593m NYANGANI

Juliasdale

2166m
Manyoli

2000m

Odzi R.

Nyakupinga R.

Pungwe View
Pungwe Falls

Buwu

Pungwe R.

Honde View

Mtarazi Falls

1956m

1880m
Mangua

Mtarazi R.

Honde R.

# Setting the scene

Nyanga, which lies to the north of Mutare in Manicaland Province, is part of the Eastern Highlands of Zimbabwe. It is a large tract of broken country with Nyanga village the administrative and commercial centre.

Relief, climate and vegetation are very varied. The beautiful gorge of the Pungwe River lies at the base of Nyangani mountain, which is the highest point in Zimbabwe at 2 593 metres. Rivers plunge over cliffs into valleys far below. There are huge bare granite domes and piled up rocks making stark and weird skylines. Thick mist gives way to warm clear sunshine. There are softly rounded grassy hills and the dense forests of the east.

## Relief and Geology

The dissected high ground of Nyanga is at a general altitude of 1800 metres above sea level. Below this height are the river valleys, the area falling away to the west and the lower slopes of the eastern escarpment. Above 1800 metres are granite domes such as Manyoli, the plateau of Troutbeck, Little Connemara and the Downs and the high dolerite edge of the eastern escarpment including Nyangani itself. This escarpment is a formidable barrier of dolerite cliffs, gorges and steep slopes which divides the high ground of Nyanga from the Honde valley in the south and the Pungwe and the Kairezi (Gairezi) valleys further north. It is at its steepest along the flanks of Nyangani with the tea estates some 1700 metres below. Where gradients are less steep paths descend to the foothills and beyond. The main Honde road is, without doubt, the most spectacular scenic drive in the country. Nyangani, a sacred mountain, wreathed in legend and mystery, has a fairly gentle north-western slope making climbing easy. The south-western face and the eastern flanks are however precipitous with typical palisaded dolerite cliffs. There are many outcrops of hard flinty hornfels.

To the south of the mountain the watershed that divides the Pungwe from the Nyangombi and the Odzi river systems is often very narrow and in places only the width of the Pungwe Scenic Drive which uses the ridge for some considerable distance. The many streams that drain the south-west of the mountain meander through grasslands forming strings of pools, ox-bows and entrenched reaches, ideal for trout. The Pungwe itself first flows south then turns to flow north-east as it plunges into the gorge. Along the edge of the escarpment there are many rapids and waterfalls; so many that they are often nameless.

The north and eastern slopes of the mountain are drained by the Kairezi and its tributaries such as the Tsanga. A vast area, mainly granite, of very rugged terrain.

To the west of the Pungwe watershed is open granite country with steep-sided but rounded ridges and valleys. From Sanyatwe to Juliasdale the scenery is much more broken. There are beautiful domes and tumbled boulder kopjes. The region is drained by the Odzi and its tributaries.

Both this area and the Pungwe catchment are marked by deep erosion gullies. These are caused by the high rainfall and the permeable nature of the colluvial soils. Water percolates downwards so the subsoil remains moist throughout the year. Weatherable material such as felspar is leached out, resulting in slumps, sink-holes and soil-slip. Although these gullies are a natural result of erosion in high rainfall mountain regions, particularly in contact zones between dolerite and granite (Bassett 1963), they are often speeded on by man's influence. Late Iron Age furrows that have been breached, cattle, horse and human paths, old roads, burning and cultivation, all play their part. The gullies heal surprisingly quickly and would provide wonderful sites for a plant-succession study.

The part of the National Park drained by the Nyangombi, Claremont Estate and Nyanga village, have a relief similar to the Odzi basin, but here there are several dolerite sheets and dykes.

To the north of Nyanga village and the National Park the land rises in a series of very steep buttresses to the high ground of Troutbeck, Little Connemara and the Downs.

The western edge of this plateau has a very distinct, often precipitous, scarp. The only break is the Bende Gap in the north.

There is a generally undulating surface with a drop in altitude from west to east and to the north.

Geologically this is the most interesting part of Nyanga. Massive granites were eroded down. Sediments of the Umkondo Group were deposited on this surface, subjected to uplift, eroded and then extensively intruded by dolerite along the bedding planes and joints. With the intense heat some sediments were metamorphosed giving rise to hard, flinty and sometimes banded hornfels. Outcrops of these rocks and the sedimentary shales and siltstones are a feature of the Troutbeck landscape today.

When the extensive dolerite sill that makes up much of the surface decomposes it gives rise to laterite: a pinkish orange spongy looking material which often occurs as a shell, enclosing the hard, fine grained unaltered rock. Laterite also occurs in a massive form. It is known as 'Nyanga Stone'; can be sawn into blocks when first exposed or when wet; and is often used for building.

Most of the plateau is drained north and north-eastward by the Kairezi River and its many tributaries.

To the west of Nyanga village and west of the high ground of Juliasdale is granite country. Out of the generally very gentle undulating surface rise dwalas (large domed rocks) and castle kopjes such as Rupurara and Dziwa. Many streams flow into the Nyangombi River.

A dolerite 'egg'

## Climate

The climate of Nyanga is as varied as the relief. Altitude and aspect are the most important factors affecting both temperature and rainfall. The eastern escarpment is, for much of its length, at right angles to the prevailing wind. This gives rise to a very high annual rainfall on the windward slopes. Gleneagles has 3 866mm and Nyazengu an unofficial mean of over 4 000mm. Areas to the lee of the mountains receive very much less. The Nyanga Experiment Station's mean is 1 120mm and the police station in the village averages 979mm. Besides this rain shadow effect, there is also a general decrease in rainfall from east to west, and from the mountains northward and southward. As an example, Sanyatwe in the south-west, has a mean of 891mm. Throughout Nyanga, the rains tend to be more reliable and the rainy season longer, than in most other parts of Zimbabwe. Early rains fall in October and the season extends through to April. January and February are usually the wettest months. In the wetter parts of the district winter rain, 'guti', and mist occur. The granite area of Juliasdale is particularly subject to hail at the start of the rains.

Early morning mist

Temperatures are much moderated by altitude. In winter heavy frost often occurs at night, especially in sheltered valleys as the cold air drains downward and becomes trapped. Valleys with steep sides may have a late sunrise and early sunset. North- and west-facing slopes are the warmest.

## Soils

The soils are closely related to the geology, but climate, slope and vegetation also play a part. Generally, soils derived from granite are sandy, pale-coloured loams, shallow in the drier areas but with deeper pockets where the rainfall is higher. Soils derived from dolerite have a higher clay content and may be brick-red on slopes, with a gravel profile close to the surface but are often black and very clayey in valleys. The subsoil is a dull pink. Where there are sedimentary rocks soils are fine-grained, red or pink. They contain mica. Much of the Kairezi basin has alluvial and colluvial soils of this type. (Stocklmayer 1978)

The amount of humus is in direct relation to the vegetation, slope and man's use of the soils over the centuries. There are pockets of true peat in soak areas where sphagnum moss has been able to grow. With the generally high rainfall, leaching occurs and most soils show a potassium and phosphorus deficiency with a low pH.

## Vegetation

There is a great diversity of natural vegetation because of the complex controlling factors of climate, relief and soils. These factors are complicated by the hand of man. There have been people in the region for many thousands of years. The earliest we know of were the San, early Stone Age hunter-gatherers. Their paintings, small friezes, have been found on the granite walls and overhangs of the kopjes, to the west of Nyanga village, within 5km north-east of the village, the higher parts of the Warrendale resettlement area, the military cantonment and in Nyamaropa. Stone Age tools have also been found in these and other places from the Kairezi valley to Bonda Mission (Payne 1990). These people are thought to have survived 'until some 300 years ago' (Garlake 1966). One cannot assess the effect on the vegetation caused by these Stone Age people or by the influx of Bantu-speakers nearly 2 000 years ago, but these early Iron Age people with their primitive tools, shifting cultivation and livestock, must have had some impact.

By about the 16th century the Iron Age farmers were well settled. Extensive areas of the uplands were terraced, sunken pits constructed to protect stock and 'forts' built. Today the ruins of these are often hidden by trees and shrubs, because of the shelter and protection from fire offered by the stones. Along the eastern escarpment, especially in the Pungwe Gorge, pits and terraces are found in dense forest. By the end of the 17th century there was a movement westward to what Summers (1958) called 'the Lowland zone'. It has been suggested that this was because the climate here was more hospitable and fruit trees such as marula (Sclerocarya birrea) grow. A vast area was cleared and the stones used to form terrace walls. Dwellings were scattered throughout the area with a partly sunken pit often central to a group of huts. There are thousands of kilometres of terracing. Garlake says that this need not indicate a large population practising intensive agriculture but rather that the fields were abandoned as fertility declined and new ones built in a type of shifting cultivation. Sutton (1983) agreed with this but on a return visit to Nyanga in 1987 found 'signs to the contrary' and says, 'Rather than regarding the terraces of Nyanga as the slowly accumulated relics of extensive or shifting cultivation, we may come to understand them better as part of a more intensive, or at least specialized, agricultural system'. He suggests that the furrows, for example, might have been designed to irrigate the tsenza beds of the valley floors. These ridged beds called 'mihomba' were built up and the tsenza planted. (Plectranthus esculentus is an indigenous plant. The roots are boiled and eaten, or eaten raw, even today.) We do not know if the people of this Nyanga culture dispersed or if they were absorbed by other peoples. Their impact on the vegetation must have been great.

By the turn of the 19th century considerable areas of the highlands had been parcelled out or bought by settlers. Rhodes acquired a vast tract of land and it is this that has formed the main part of what is now Nyanga National Park.

Today most of the land outside the two parks is used for commercial timber, fruit, potatoes, holiday homes and tourist resorts.

In spite of man's long use of the land it is still possible to discern a natural pattern of vegetation.

## Moist evergreen forests

These are the magnificent climax forests of the eastern escarpment. The canopy is closed with only a few trees emerging above the general level.

Where trees have fallen and along streams the shrub and the herb layers are dense with moss, epiphytes such as ferns and orchids; lianas, fungi and lichens cover the trees. Most trees have straight trunks and branches about two-thirds of the way up. They are seldom buttressed.

The outer edges of these forests are difficult to penetrate as there are tangled masses of wild bamboo (Oxytenanthera abyssinica) and a rank climbing fern Lygodium kerstenii. Where these forests have been disturbed muzhanje (Uapaca kirkiana) and Albizia gummifera are often common trees. Some of the dominant trees of the forests are:

| | |
|---|---|
| Anthocleista grandiflora | forest big leaf |
| Filicium decipiens | fern leaf |
| Khaya nyasica | red mahogany |
| Maranthes goetzeniana | maranthes |
| Newtonia buchananii | forest newtonia |
| Pachystela brevipes | pachystela |
| Xylopia parviflora | forest red-fingers |

Opening from inside a pit

## Moist broad leaf forests

Above 1500m the forest of the eastern slopes of Nyanga have a more open canopy so both the shrub and herb storey are denser. Lianas are uncommon but orchids, mosses, fungi and lichens drape the trees. There are many ferns including beautiful stands of spiny tree fern (Cyathea manniana) and forest tree ferns (Cyathea capensis) along the stream banks. In clearings are colonies of dragon trees (Dracaena steudneri, and wild bananas (Ensete ventricosum).

In the forests are many different species of trees and a fascinating altitudinal change can be seen when walking down a forest path. The most noticeable trees are those that emerge above the canopy such as the parasol tree (Polyscias fulva) and false cabbage tree (Schefflera umbellifera) with its loose heads of yellow flowers from February to April. Other trees include:

| | |
|---|---|
| Ilex mitis | african holly (with its load of epiphytes) |
| Macaranga capensis | spiny macaranga |
| Macaranga mellifera | forest macaranga |
| Psychotria zombamontana | psychotria (which forms an under-storey) |
| Schrebera alata | wing-leaved wooden pear |
| Tabernaemontana stapfiana | soccer ball fruit tree |
| Trimeria grandiflora | mulberry leaf trimeria |

These broad leaf forests are suffering encroachment as the pressure of population increases in the Honde valley. Burning to extend grazing areas, collection of timber for fuel and building and clearing for crops such as coffee have all taken their toll. The forests themselves resist fire but the edges are opened up, allowing easier access for exploitation.

Forests of a similar type occur in the valleys at the headwaters of the west-flowing rivers, sheltered valleys and slopes within the Pungwe catchment basin. The trees are not as tall and the canopy is more open, so extensive stands of ferns are found. The outer edges of these forests may be protected by a dense tangle of bracken (Pteridium aquilinum) and brambles (Rubus rigidus).

These forests have been severely reduced by fire and the planting of commercial trees such as pine and wattle.

*Polyscias fulva*

## Dry conifer forests

*Even more susceptible to fire are the forests of the rocky outcrops and steep-sided river valleys such as Mare and Nyamziwa below the falls.*

*These dry conifer forests of the mountains, as classified by* Flora Zambesiaca 1967, *are usually surrounded by grasslands, so are vulnerable. Typical trees of these relic forests include:*

| | | | |
|---|---|---|---|
| Ilex mitis | *african holly* | Widdringtonia nodiflora | *mulanje-cedar* |
| Podocarpus latifolius | *real yellowwood* | Xymalos monospora | *lemonwood* |
| Schefflera umbellifera | *false cabbage tree* | | |

Widdringtonia *is the only representative of the cypress family indigenous to Zimbabwe with the exception of one known specimen of African pencil-cedar* (Juniperus procera) *growing in a crevice between high boulders on a granite mountain west of Nyanga village.*

*The transition from forest to grassland is often gradual. Shrubs such as St John's wort* (Hypericum revolutum), *which may be up to 4 metres in height, grow in extensive stands. There are also areas where* Stoebe vulgaris *and petrol bush* (Erica spp.) *flourish. Mosses, lycopodiums and ferns such as Nyanga fern* (Asplenium aethiopicum) *and bracken cover the ground. There are isolated grassy patches, mainly on hilltops. Much of this shrub vegetation has been cleared for pine and wattle. Many valley floors are also shrub covered.* Leucosidea sericea *is reputed to indicate a stream suitable for trout. (See illustration overleaf.)*

## Woodland

*The only true woodland occurs in the granite areas of the west. Here musasa* (Brachystegia spiciformis) *is the dominant tree. The distribution of the musasa woodland is affected by a number of physical factors such as soil depth, wind and ground temperatures (Thomson 1974).*

*Population pressure has also been a factor as much of the musasa woodlands have been occupied intermittently for thousands of years. It was not until 1962 that the last people were moved out of the National Park.*

*The most favourable areas are on gentle north- and west-facing slopes where soils are well drained and deep. As the altitudinal limit of about 2 000m is reached, where the slope is steep or where soils are thin, the trees become dwarfed and gnarled. It has been suggested (Rattry 1963) that these trees should be considered a subspecies but it seems that seed taken from these dwarf trees when germinated and planted in favourable conditions would develop into trees of a normal height.*

Leaves of the juniper tree

Within the musasa woodland there are comparatively few other species of trees. These include wild figs (Ficus spp.), *lucky bean trees* (Erythrina latissima *and* E. lysistemon), *cabbage trees* (Cussonia spicata), *and species of* protea *and* faurea. *Where soils are deep and clayey there are colonies of the beautiful Nyanga flat-top* Acacia abyssinica. *Many herbs have a woody rootstock which enables them to resist fire.*

*Leucosidea sericea*

*Ficus thonningii*

## Grasslands

*Much of Nyanga is grass covered. Between the watershed of the eastern escarpment and the woodlands of the granites, from the foot of Nyangani to the Pungwe Gorge and to Nyanga village are grassy rolling hills. Where there are rocky outcrops and along streams there may be groups of trees and shrubs. Often such clumps of trees will be around an ancient pit structure. In the upper reaches of the Pungwe River and middle Matenderere valley strange anomalous circular patches of shrubs and herbs can be clearly seen. These circles are about 11 to 15 metres in diameter. The long-time officer in charge of the Nyanga Experiment Station, Bud Payne, said: 'Dr Oliver West examined the vegetation and arranged for soil analyses to be carried out in order to elucidate the problem'. A trench dug right across a patch showed the honeycomb structure typical of a termite mound, but unfortunately, no results of the investigation have been published.*

*Where the grass has been disturbed in other places bracken and* Helichysum splendidum *take over. Ancient fields can be picked out from a distance, in fact even from aerial photographs, by the presence of these plants and the grass* Eragrostis acraea. *In the drier west* Hyparrhenia cymbaria *is the grass of disused fields. Some of the dominant grasses are:*

| | |
|---|---|
| Digitaria gazensis | Hyparrhenia newtonii |
| Digitaria nitens | Loudetia simplex |
| Eragrostis racemosa | Themeda triandra |

*Typical trees are:*

| | |
|---|---|
| Cussonia spicata | *mountain cabbage tree* |
| Erythrina latissima | *broad-leaved lucky bean* |
| Erythrina lysistemon | *eastern district lucky bean* |
| Ficus natalensis | *natal fig* |
| Ficus sur | *cape fig* |
| Ficus thonningii | *wild fig* |
| Prunus africana | *bitter almond* |

*Ficus sur*

A second grassland area is the almost treeless downs of the plateau. Here the grass is tussocky and interspersed with aromatic herbs and low shrubs. Unfortunately, much of this grassy upland has been invaded by self-seeded pine and wattle. Kikuyu grass, introduced from Kenya in the 'thirties, has also become invasive.

Some of the dominant grasses are:

Alloteropsis semialata

Cymbopogon caesius *(where the rainfall is very high)*

Loudetia simplex

Monocymbium ceresiiforme

Setaria sphacelata

Themeda triandra

Nyangani and the plateau to the north of the summit have true mountain grassland. The grasses are tussocky with low growing plants in between. Where drainage is poor sedges (Cyperaceae) take over.

Many people think that in past times much of Nyanga was forested, and there is visible evidence of deforestation in the musasa region and the forests of the eastern escarpment. There is, however, nothing at all to indicate that the grasslands of

*Cussonia spicata*
leaf and flower buds

the Pungwe basin, the plateau or the Downs, were ever wooded. Tomlinson (1973) concludes: 'Grasslands of the plateau are not the product of clearance of woodlands by man. Studies of pollen have shown that even 12 000 years ago there were very few trees in these areas now occupied by grasslands.'

## Conservation

There are approximately 21 700 hectares under commercial timber. Strict management is carried out. Fires are controlled, cutting and replanting carefully planned. Outside the bounds of the big estates, however, both pine and wattle have become a threat to the indigenous vegetation as they spread to many areas including the national parks. These 'runaway' exotics are difficult to eradicate. Fire stimulates the germination of seeds so is of little help except to destroy adult pine. Biological control may be the answer in the future but at present mechanical or hand clearing is the only practical solution. If every landowner could check the spread of aliens on his own land perhaps those growing on state and unoccupied land could be removed by 'hack groups' of interested people or organizations.

*Mariscus hemisphaericus*

Another problem, a related one, is fire control: 'to burn or not to burn'. Consensus is that controlled fires at regular intervals are preferable to the almost inevitable accidental fires which race through the vegetation, destroying or damaging plants and animals because of the intense heat as the tangled cover burns. Most plants are able to survive if the burn is early enough in the dry season. Winter rains also bring through enough growth to prevent sheet erosion of the exposed soil. The Nyanga intensive conservation area committee has drawn up a very comprehensive fire plan (1989). Every landowner should make sure all regulations are abided by. No vegetation should be set alight without permission from the fire warden of the zone. If you are a visitor never light a fire that might get away, never leave coals smouldering, never discard lighted cigarettes or matches and remember bottles act as magnifying glasses in the sunlight.

Where there are beautiful flowers it is human nature to pick armfuls and dig up plants to take home. How much more rewarding it is to see them in bloom against a background of yellow grass and the clear blue sky of the Nyanga mountains. Before you pick or collect, ask yourself whether it is 'necessary, desirable or useful'. Wouldn't it be better to photograph or paint or draw the plant? Why not try growing an indigenous plant you 'have to have' from a seed or spore? It is most rewarding.

In Zimbabwe, as in most countries of the world, there is legislation to protect indigenous plants. People are generally aware of regulations governing the protection of fauna but few, it would seem, know about those pertaining to flora.

*A brief summary of the*
# NATIONAL PARKS AND WILDLIFE ACT 14 OF 1975
(As amended at 1st August, 1990)

**Section 15** : No person shall pick any plant in a National Park.

Penalties: (For a first conviction)—Not more than $2 000 or imprisonment for a period not exceeding 2 years or both.

**Sections 38–43**: *Specially Protected Indigenous Plants:*

No person, subject to certain provisions, shall pick any specially protected indigenous plant.

Penalties: (First conviction)—Not more than $1 500 or imprisonment of not more than 18 months or both.

No person shall sell any specially protected indigenous plant without a permit, or unless he is a dealer, etc.

Penalties: (First conviction)—Not more than $1 000 or imprisonment for a period not exceeding 12 months or both.

No person shall purchase a specially protected plant except from a person who is a holder of a permit, etc.

Penalties: (First conviction)—Not more than $1 000 or imprisonment for a period not exceeding 12 months or both.

The Seventh Schedule of the Act includes the following specially protected indigenous plants:

| Botanical name | Common name | Botanical name | Common name |
| --- | --- | --- | --- |
| *Cyrtanthus* – all species | fire lilies | *Aloe* – all species and | |
| *Dierama* – all species | hairbells | natural hybrids | aloes |
| *Adenium multiflorum* | save star | *Encephalartos* – all species | cycads |
| *Borassus aethiopum* | borassus palm | *Gloriosa superba* | flame lily |
| *Raphia farinifera* | raffia palm | *Platycerium alcicorne* | staghorn fern |
| *Juniperus procera* | african juniper | All species of *epiphytic* | |
| *Cyathea* – all species tree ferns | | (or *lithophytic*) orchids | orchids |

In addition, Government Notice No. 353 of 1978 Parks and Wildlife (Protected Indigenous Plants) (Inyanga) Notice, lists the following as protected plants within the area of the land for which the Inyanga Intensive Conservation Area Committee has been appointed the conservation committee:

| Botanical name | Common name |
| --- | --- |
| *Scadoxus multiflorus* | blood lily |
| *Dierama* spp. | hairbells |
| *Cyrtanthus rhodesianus* | fire lily |
| *Protea caffra* | manica protea |
| *Widdringtonia nodiflora* | mountain cedar |
| *Helichrysum adenocarpum* | pink everlasting |
| *Kniphofia linearifolia* | red-hot poker |
| *Securidaca longipedunculata* | violet tree |

**Sections 44–46**: *Indigenous Plants (not in National Parks)*

No person shall, without reasonable excuse, pick any indigenous plant, on any land other than his own without a permit from the land owner or appropriate authority.

Penalties: (First conviction) Not more than $1 000 or imprisonment not exceeding 1 year or both.

FINES of less than $100 may be imposed by National Parks officials without the matter being taken to Court.

# January

## – in the wet

GESNERIACEÆ

## *Streptocarpus umtalensis*
blue flowered *Nyangani* form
(actual size)

*This genus is well represented in the Nyanga area. A number of species flourish in the damp shelter of the forests and by streams and under the boulders of the granite country.*

Streptocarpus umtalensis *has a single tongue-like velvety leaf up to 30cm long. The flower stem bears a cluster of violet-blue flowers followed by the twisted seed pods that give it the name* 'streptocarpus'. *These plants grow near rocks in the wet forests of the escarpment.*

*The white form of* Streptocarpus umtalensis *is found at lower altitudes and is illustrated on page 65.*

## *Chironia gratissima*

(50cm)   GENTIANACEÆ

There are four species of Chironia in Zimbabwe. Chironia gratissima *can be recognized as the flower matures, by the bright yellow twisted anthers. It is found growing near streams, in seepage areas, and where water collects during the rains. Great patches of vivid colour brighten the poorly-drained areas of Nyangani and the headwaters of the Pungwe River.*

## Oberonia disticha

(specially protected plant)

ORCHIDACEÆ

The magnificent climax forests of the eastern slopes of Mount Nyangani and of the Pungwe gorge often form a closed canopy where the only gaps are caused by fallen trees.

Mosses, lichens, ferns, orchids and other epiphytes grow in great profusion.

Oberonia disticha *has yellowish-green fleshy leaves arranged in an overlapping pattern. The insignificant pale straw-coloured flowers emerge from the leaves in a 7—8 centimetre-long hanging inflorescence.*

The granite area of Juliasdale from Crusader (Chinaka) to Susu rumba and Manyoli and from there to Punch Rock, the Canyon and through to London Store, has a wealth of trees, flowers and other plants not found in the more exposed areas of the Downs o the escarpment.

In the sheltered valleys between the great bare domes o granite around Juliasdale are stands of Brachystegia spiciformis and Acacia abyssinica. The grass is tall and there are many flowers

The white spider lily is sweet-scented and, as with man white flowers, the perfume is strongest in the evening and attracts moths.

The flowers of Radinosiphon leptostachya are almost orchid-like The plant grows up to 50cm in height.

Most Asclepiads, like Glossostelma carsonii, have a milky sap and seeds with silky hairs. (See also page 147.)

*Glossostelma carsonii*

(50cm)    ASCLEPIADACEÆ

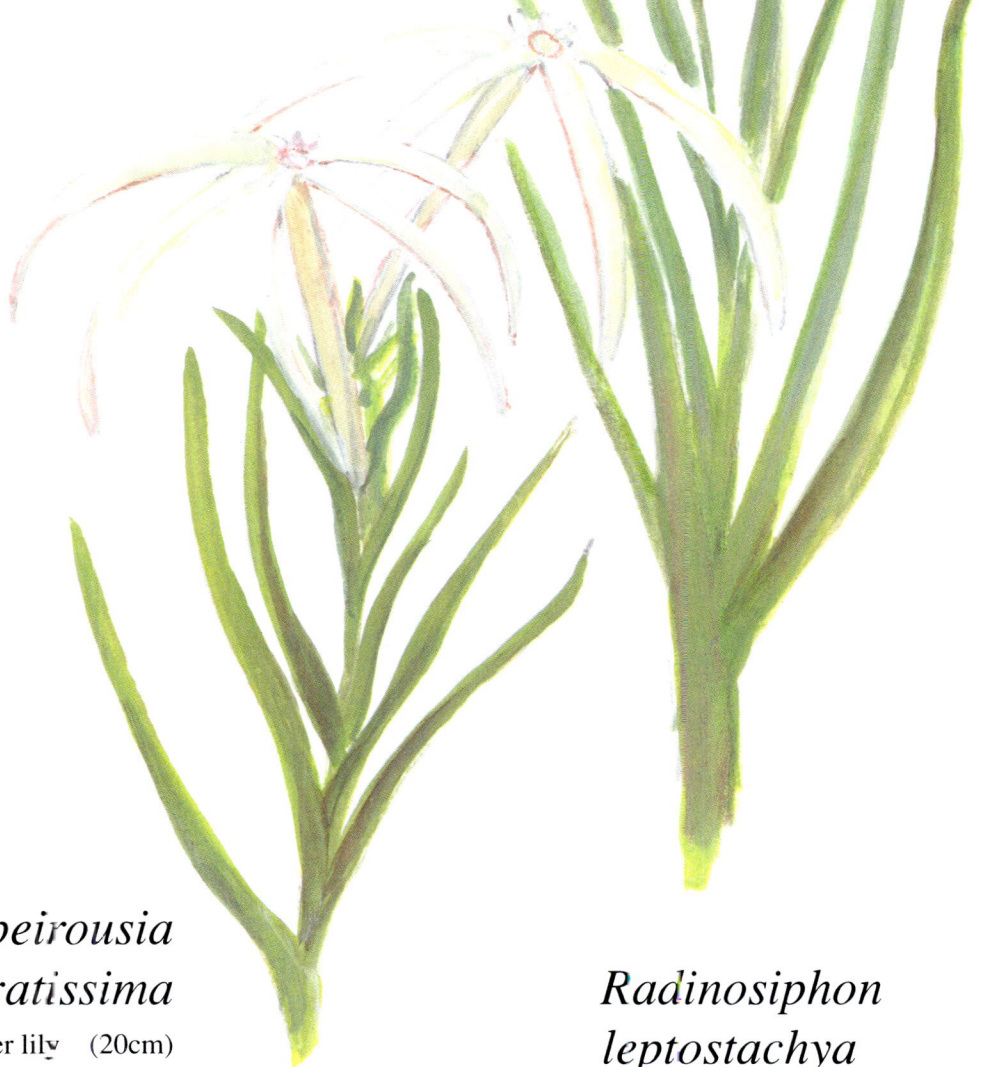

*Lapeirousia
odoratissima*

spider lily    (20cm)

IRIDACEÆ

*Radinosiphon
leptostachya*

(50cm)    IRIDACEÆ

## Schizostylis coccinea

scarlet river-lily          (25cm)

IRIDACEÆ

*The flowers seem to glisten with a crystalline sparkle and are a beautiful sight along the banks of streams and rivers.*

*At the Pungwe drift they grow in the grass along the river's edge and even in the sand right near the water, sheltered by a rock from the wash.*

*Because these flowers are so striking they are often picked and every year there are fewer to be found.*

## Satyrium trinerve

(50cm)　　ORCHIDACEÆ

Orchids are one of the largest and most complex of all plant families.

　　The orchid flower is irregular but with a balanced symmetry. There are usually three sepals, two petals and a lip which is a petal but different to the other two. Most orchids have spurs. The stamen and the pistil are joined to form a column which holds the pollinia which is made up of a mass of pollen grains.

　　The Satyrium trinerve illustrated here was found growing near Juliasdale. The species is easily recognized as the flower-bracts, which are attached to the ovary, are very long and stand away from the stem.

## Satyrium longicauda
## Disa versicolor

(30cm)

ORCHIDACEÆ

There are 19 species of Satyrium and 20 species of Disa in Zimbabwe. Satyrium flowers have twin spurs and usually the lip is uppermost and forms the hood. The ovary is not twisted. Disa flowers usually have only one spur which is often horizontal or ascending. The ovary is twisted. Satyrium longicauda grows in the open grasslands of the mist belt above 1800m. It may be pure white to pink and is sweetly scented. Great fields of this orchid can be found in the Troutbeck area. Disa versicolor, as the name suggests, may be deep pink, purple, cerise or red; fading as the flowers mature. It is often found side by side with Satyrium longicauda.

## Cynorkis hanningtonii

(15cm)                    ORCHIDACEÆ

*Species of* Cynorkis *have one or two shiny leaves and the flowers are white, purple or lilac. They grow in the shade of forest or plantations and are more widespread in tropical Africa than in the more temperate zones to the south.*

## Habenaria clavata

(70cm)   ORCHIDACEÆ

*Habenarias have green or green and white flowers and many have a spidery appearance because the petals and the lip are divided and elongated.*

*Habenaria clavata grows to up to 70cm tall and is found in the open grasslands below 2 000m in altitude. The flowers have a sweet scent and it is this that attracts one's attention. Being green it is difficult to see in the green grass at this time of year.*

## Clematopsis villosa

shock-headed peter (1m) RANUNCULACEÆ

*This plant grows throughout the highveld of Zimbabwe.*

*The colour of the flower may vary from a creamy white through to pink. It is easy to recognize with its droopy flower heads.*

*This plant is a perennial and may be up to a metre in height so that the flowers are above the top of the grass. It grows in the Juliasdale area and around Nyanga village but not along the wet escarpment.*

① *Chlorophytum colubrinum*
  (1m)   ANTHERICACEÆ

② *Chlorophytum* sp.
  (80cm)   ANTHERICACEÆ

④ *Huernia hislopii* subsp. *hislopii*
  (10cm)   ASCLEPIADACEÆ

③ *Aeollanthus rehmannii*
  (20cm)   LAMIACEÆ

*This group of plants was found growing in the rich soil between granite boulders near Juliasdale.*

   Huernia hislopii *is found throughout Zimbabwe in granite areas. The plant is leafless with five angled stems.*

# Polystachya ottoniana
### (8cm)      ORCHIDACEÆ

*Polystachyas are epiphytic or lithophytic orchids and are widespread throughout the Nyanga district. They have pseudobulbs bearing one or two leaves. The flower stems rise from the tip of the pseudobulbs. The flowers, like Satyriums, have the lip uppermost so the ovary is not twisted.*

*Polystachya ottoniana usually has two leaves per pseudobulb. These pseudobulbs are conical and joined together like a string of beads under branches or on trunks of trees in the forest.*

(specially protected plant)

## *Polystachya cultriformis*

(15cm)                    ORCHIDACEÆ

(specially protected plant)

*The* Polystachya cultriformis *illustrated here was found growing in the forests of the Pungwe gorge.*

## Eulophia odontoglossa

(40cm)     ORCHIDACEÆ

A very erect, showy orchid of the Brachystegia woodland areas.

Most striking is the deep egg-yolk yellow colour with the darker red-brown papillae on the lip.

Eulophia is the largest genus of orchids in Zimbabwe with over 60 species. They even grow in the dry south-west of the country as well as the eastern districts. The leaves of Eulophia odontoglossa are bright green and pleated and, unlike many other orchids, develop with the flower so that they are fully grown when flowering takes place.

## Eulophia nigricans

(20cm)     ORCHIDACEÆ

The leaves are either absent or only partly grown when this eulophia flowers.

## Disa saxicola

(30cm)  ORCHIDACEÆ

Towering above Nyanga village are the huge buttresses of Chera, World's View and Rukotso. The summits are wind-swept grasslands, with trees and shrubs only where shelter is provided by rocky outcrops. Between the boulders plants cluster taking advantage of the run-off of moisture, accumulations of leaf mould and protection from fire.

Disa saxicola is found in mossy cracks between rocks and is easily distinguished by the purple spots on the hood of the flowers. The flower illustrated is unusually dark in colour. They are often a pale lilac or almost white but all have the purple spots and dark spur.

## Eucomis autumnalis

pineapple lily, chifuro (40cm)
HYACINTHACEÆ

Eucomis autumnalis *has soft fleshy leaves with undulate edges. The inflorescence which resembles a pineapple has greeny flowers and is topped by a tuft of bracts. The plant dies down completely in the winter but as the large bulbs are close to the surface they are often exposed when cultivation takes place. The pineapple lily grows throughout the highveld of Zimbabwe.*

## Scadoxus pole-evansii

nyanga fire-ball    (1m)
AMARYLLIDACEÆ

*Endemic to the Pungwe and Mtarazi areas, these magnificent flowers make an unforgettable sight in the dappled shade of the montane forests.*

*In favourable areas, hundreds of plants grow with ferns and as the fruit, when ripe, is eaten by both vervet and samango monkeys as well as forest birds like green louries, the seeds are spread. Plants in flower have been found on rocks and even high above the ground in humus-filled forks of trees.*

## Gladiolus dalenii

tsonga

(1m) IRIDACEÆ

This flower grows in most areas of Zimbabwe except above 2 000m and in the very dry lowveld.

The flowers may be plain orange, as they are in the Plumtree area, or yellow or speckled with fine lines, as they are in the eastern districts.

The plant is a perennial which grows from a corm which produces many offsets. When in flower they stand out clearly against the grass and are a fine sight.

This gladiolus is possibly one of the plants that was used to produce the cultivated hybrids and is well worth a place in the garden.

# February

## – orchids in bloom

## Satyrium chlorocorys

(30cm)　　　ORCHIDACEÆ

There are two extensive areas of very high ground to the south-east and the north-west of Troutbeck. Here the grass is short because of the temperate climate and the often shallow soils. In favourable areas great fields of orchids are in bloom at this time of year.

The specimen of Satyrium chlorocorys illustrated here was found close to St. Catherine's Church and is actual size. The following week many were found in the Connemara area and they were much taller (up to 30cm). Note how Satyrium can be recognized by the flower-bracts.

The Nyanga Downs, as the name implies, is a gently rolling area of over 2 000m. It is doleritic and many of the streams rise from soaks, not valley soaks as in the Pungwe, but areas of shallow soil over sheet rock.

These three species of Iridaceae are from such a location.

Moraea spathulata also grows on the south-western slopes of Mount Nyangani and even if the flowers are not found the persistent, decorative seed heads may be recognized. Both these moraeas are toxic to cattle and other stock.

Crocosmia aurea grows near water, sometimes at high altitudes in the open, but often in the deep shade near forest streams. The birds love the orange fruit which has a dark seed.

### ① Moraea spathulata
yellow moraea (1m) IRIDACEÆ
### ② Moraea carsonii
blue moraea (30cm) IRIDACEÆ
### ③ Crocosmia aurea
wild montbretia (50cm) IRIDACEÆ

① ② ③

## Bidens formosa
cosmos (2,5m) ASTERACEÆ

## Lilium formosanum
(2,5m)    LILIACEÆ

*These are invaders. Cosmos grows only at the lower altitudes while the lilies have become widely naturalized except where frosts are severe.*

## Momordica foetida

(fruit actual size)
CUCURBITACEÆ

A light creeper with heart-shaped leaves and creased, creamy-apricot coloured flowers with a black and orange throat.

A fruit splits open into three segments revealing the very shiny red-fleshed seed. It is often found scrambling over thickets of shrubs below 1800m.

In spite of the unpleasant smell the leaves are sometimes cooked and eaten as a vegetable.

# *Kniphofia linearifolia*

(specially protected plant) red-hot poker, musundu

# *Kniphofia splendida*

ASPHODELACEÆ

*The red-hot poker grows along the watershed from north of Harare to Mutare and the Eastern Highlands. The leaves are keel-shaped and about a metre long. The flower heads are compact and usually not more than 12cm long. The stamens are hardly visible. Often found in swampy areas but also in long grass and thickets of low shrubs.*

*Kniphofia splendida is the only other Zimbabwe red-hot poker and grows only in the Nyanga and Chimanimani areas. The plant is larger and tougher than Kniphofia linearifolia. Fibre from within the leaves is made into a very strong twisted twine used for nets. The flowers have extended stamens. The one illustrated here is an unusual yellow form found in a soak area in the upper Pungwe valley.*

*Gladiolus gracillimus*

IRIDACEÆ
(1m) tsonga

*Gladiolus masukuensis*

These are later flowering than Gladiolus
dalenii *(see page 38): perhaps it is
because they grow at higher altitudes.*
    Gladiolus masukuensis *is found in the
Troutbeck area while* Gladiolus gracillimus
*occurs above 1800m. This plant seeds readily
and the seed capsules on slender stems are an
eye-catching sight as the grass begins to turn
at the end of the rains. Both of these plants
are good garden subjects.*

*Habenaria subaequalis*

(28cm)    ORCHIDACEÆ

*Schizochilus cecilii*

(22cm)    ORCHIDACEÆ

*These orchids were found growing in the shallow peat-like soils of Rukotso, the second highest mountain in Zimbabwe at 2404 metres.*

*Habenaria subaequalis has a sweet but rather sickly smell.*

*Schizochilus cecilii has minute yellow-white flowers arranged in a tight spiral around the flower stem.*

## Streptocarpus eylesii

(20cm)          GESNERIACEÆ

Streptocarpus eylesii *grows in granite areas, particularly in the musasa woodland of Julias-dale. The single leaf may be 20 to 30cm long and, as its tip dies back each dry season, it may take from two to four years to reach the flowering stage. Once the plant seeds, it dies.*

*A group of these plants clustered under the drip-line of a huge grey granite boulder or growing on a bare bank is a pleasing sight.*

## Streptocarpus pumilus

(actual size)       GESNERIACEÆ

*Colonies of these tiny flowers grow in the caves and over-hangs of Susurumba.*

## *Sopubia mannii*

(40cm) SCROPHULARIACEÆ

Sopubia mannii *grows in many areas of Zimbabwe from Gokwe to Hwange and from Zimbabwe to Shurugwi and the highveld through to the Eastern Highlands. It grows from a woody perennial rootstock which is able to withstand the fiercest grass-fires. The specimen shown here was found growing in the grass at the Honde viewpoint.*

## Disa patula var. transvaalensis

(60cm)                          ORCHIDACEÆ

This disa is tall and slender. The flowers have a long ascending spur and may be pink or a dull mauve. They grow in the open grasslands of the Nyanga Downs and on the slopes of Nyangani.

## Disa ochrostachya                 ORCHIDACEÆ

golden candle orchid (1m)

Another disa of Troutbeck and the Downs is Disa ochrostachya or golden candle orchid with its striking yellow flowers with orange markings. Groups of these orchids grow on the hills of Kwaraguza.

FUNGI    (actual size)
① *Amanita muscaria*    fly agaric
② *Boletus edulis*        dindindi
③ *Collybia* sp.
④ *Dictyophora indusiata*
⑤ *Macrolepiota zeyheri*
⑥ *Scleroderma cepa*
⑦ *Tremella* sp.

*This group of fungi was collected in an hour's walk through pine plantations and indigenous forest in the Pungwe area. The rainfall season is usually taken from the 1st October and in that year by the end of February stood at 2 148mm. The turquoise blue fungi on the upright wood, and the green, glow in the dusk with phosphorescent light. The red spotted* Amanita muscaria *known as fly agaric is an exotic which grows mainly under pines but may sometimes be found under other trees. It is very poisonous with the first symptoms appearing after about half an hour.*

# Clathrus archeri

red stinkhorn  **BASIDIOMYCETES**

*Most fungi live on decayed organic material. Tiny hair-like threads called hyphae thrust into the material making up a mat known as mycelium. It is this that produces the 'eggs' of the stinkhorns.*

*When the 'eggs' split open the fruit-body of the stinkhorn emerges. Five to seven tentacles joined at the tips grow upwards but as they mature they separate to open like petals. The tentacles have patches of shiny black substance which emits a foul smell like rotting meat.*

*Cynorkis kassneriana*  (actual size)

*For over two months it had been fascinating watching the growth of single glossy green leaves with a purple under-surface on the carpets of pine needles beneath* Pinus patula.

*At last they are in bloom. Nowhere in the indigenous forest have such similar vast colonies been found.* Cynorkis kassneriana *has found an ideal habitat in the shelter of exotic trees. Neither as widespread nor in the same numbers, are* Disperis virginalis *and* Disperis anthoceros *shown here, but they grow in the same environment. Both species of* Disperis *have also been found in wattle plantations and also on the edge of the forests.*

*Disperis virginalis*

*Disperis anthoceros*

## Liparis bowkeri
(15cm)

## Stenoglottis fimbriata
(14cm)

These two orchids are from the forests of the escarpment. They may both be found growing on branches, in forks of trees, on moss covered rocks or on mossy banks on the forest floor. The flowers of Liparis bowkeri are almost translucent yellowish green. The leaves, up to 10cm long, are a very glossy green. Stenoglottis fimbriata has a basal rosette of dark green leaves from which the flower stem rises. The flowers are a beautiful lilac with darker spots on the lip.

## Piper capense

wild pepper, musatsate  (3m)                                    PIPERACEÆ

*Although not as common as in the Vumba this shrub grows in the forests of the escarpment and may sometimes reach up to four metres. The leaves are a very dark glossy green and are quilted with the veins indented on the upper surface and standing out clearly on the paler under-surface. The small white flowers are in a spike which hangs down. When the berries are ripe they turn black and can be used as a condiment. This species is closely related to* Piper nigrum *from which commercial pepper, both black and white, is obtained.*

# March

## – the purple hills

① *Striga elegans*
(20cm)

② *Craterostigma lanceolatum*
(3cm)

③ *Craterostigma plantagineum*
(3cm)

④ *Zaluzianskya* sp.
drumsticks (30cm)

*Rukotso mountain is exposed and cold. There is short mountain grass and great areas of bare sheet rock. The only shelter is provided by tumbled boulders. In the cracks and crevices are many small plants like those illustrated here. Striga elegans is parasitic on grass roots and the vivid, almost luminous scarlet flowers are made even more startling by yellow throats.*

*Craterostigma lanceolatum and Craterostigma plantagineum are related to the mopani violet of Matabeleland. These tiny plants form carpets in the shallow soil pockets in the sheet rocks. They often flower with the first rains but will continue throughout the summer.*

*In favourable areas Zaluzianskya sp. may be 30cm high, but it is often more compact. The shape of the buds give the common name drumsticks. The flowers are maroon and white.*

SCROPHULARIACEÆ

## Dierama inyangense

nyanga hairbell   (2m)   IRIDACEÆ

*This beautiful flower also grows in the shelter provided by rocks at high altitudes. Tall and very graceful it is much sought after as a garden subject, which is why it has been declared a specially protected plant. The genus* Dierama *has recently been revised by O. M. Hilliard and B. L. Burt of the Royal Botanic Garden, Edinburgh. This is the largest and most robust of the four species to be found in Zimbabwe.*

## Impatiens psychadelphoides      Impatiens sylvicola
busy lizzies (1m)      BALSAMINACEÆ      (40cm)

*Both these plants are soft perennials of the high rainfall forest edge and stream banks and are drought and frost sensitive.*

    Impatiens psychadelphoides *may be over a metre high and the flowers, although not as numerous as those of* Impatiens sylvicola, *are much larger. The seed capsule when ripe may be up to 2cm long and will burst open when touched, a feature common to all balsams.*

    Impatiens sylvicola *grows to about 40cm in height and its stems and leaves are a delicate green. The flowers are a purple-pink with maroon markings. The petals have tails and the hooded sepal has a marked spur. This plant seeds prolifically.*

## *Begonia sonderiana*

(50cm)         BEGONIACEÆ

Begonia sonderiana *grows in the forests usually near streams or boulders. A delicate plant that dies down in the winter. The decorative leaves are asymmetrically five-lobed with an irregular margin. This is one of the most beautiful flowers of Nyanga.*

## Protea caffra

chinhendere (6m) PROTEACEÆ
(specially protected plant)

*Growing on the mountain slopes within the mist belt, this small gnarled tree is often subjected to fires and the blackened branches and dead seed-heads are a feature of the mountain landscape. When in bloom, from October through to April, it is a beautiful sight. The colour of the outer bracts is whitish-green or brown-white. The inner bracts may be pale pink to rose coloured as illustrated here. As the dead flower heads do not fall off, the tree is untidy looking. The protea is sometimes known as the manica protea and is protected under that name.*

# Dissotis canescens

ruhororo  (1,5 m)          MELASTOMATACEÆ

*This dissotis grows along the watershed from Harare to Mutare and throughout the Eastern Highlands. It also occurs in the Bikita and Great Zimbabwe areas.*

*A beautiful flower of the soak areas and along river banks or anywhere where its feet can be wet. During winter it dies back as it is often found in frost-prone areas. With the first rains it grows again. The flowers are a bright magenta in contrast to the red stems and calyces.*

## Blaeria friesii
(30cm) ERICACEÆ

This is the 'heath' or 'heather' that makes the purple hills of March over vast tracts of the National Park and of the Downs.

Its flowering period is very short – often only a few days – as a heavy fall of rain will turn the flowers cinnamon-brown. The plant is a perennial and may form extensive stands often mixed with bracken and also Helichrysum splendidum.

As blaeria seeds readily it is spreading and each year new patches appear particularly after fire has swept an area.

① *Tridactyle bicaudata*
② *Brownleea maculata*
③ *Polystachya concreta*
④ *Angraecopsis parviflora*

This collection of orchids was found in the Pungwe gorge.

Tridactyle bicaudata *has long straggling stems firmly fixed to the branches or trunks of trees. The flowers are in two distinct rows.*

Polystachya concreta *has 20cm-long ovoid pseudobulbs with two or three narrowly elliptic leaves. The inflorescence is long (35cm) and the flowers are a greenish-yellow.*

Brownleea maculata *is a neat plant with the deep green glossy leaf typical of many forest orchids.*

(Specially protected plants)

## Sebaea longicaulis

(80cm)   GENTIANACEÆ

## Hebenstretia oatesii subsp. *inyangana*

(1m)   SCROPHULARIACEÆ

Sebaea longicaulis *with its bright yellow flowers catches the eye as the grass begins to brown. The plant often falls over or leans against other plants. The flowers right themselves so they face upward in spite of the prostrate stems.*

*The flowers only open in full sunlight. The leaves are arranged in a very simple decorative pattern.*

Hebenstretia oatesii subsp. inyangana *is a perennial on rocky mountain slopes mainly in dolerite areas. The flower heads are dense and the bright orange dots on the showy white flowers make it easy to recognize.*

## Aerangis mystacidii

(specially protected plant)    ORCHIDACEÆ

The Mtarazi forests have a wealth of orchids, both terrestrial and epiphytic. Unfortunately, many large trees have died or are losing branches. It is a sad sight to see a pile of firewood set aside for picnickers with orchids and epiphytic ferns still clinging to the wood.

Aerangis mysticidii is one of the most beautiful of our epiphytes as each inflorescence bears up to fifteen white flowers with long curving spurs set with precision on either side of the flower stem.

The white-flowered Streptocarpus umtalensis occurs in the same area. (See page 22.)

# Disa fragrans

## Brownleea parviflora

(35cm)          ORCHIDACEÆ   (40cm)

Disa fragrans *is 35cm tall with leaves that have a reddish-purple bar around the sheath. The flower is mottled and very sweet scented. This disa may continue blooming as late as May when most terrestrial orchids have already set seed. The seed, which is as fine as dust particles, is dispersed by wind. It is only where fungus suitable to that particular orchid is present that this seed will germinate as the young plant cannot feed itself until it produces leaves.*

*Brownleea parviflora is a very delicate orchid found growing in the grass in full sun. The inflorescence is densely packed with tiny white flowers. The single spur of each flower is purple in colour and sharply recurved like a baboon's tail.*

## Drosera burkeana
sundew (4cm) DROSERACEÆ
## Thelypteris confluens
(25cm) PTERIDOPHYTA

Drosera burkeana *is a carnivorous plant that grows in wet places throughout the Nyanga area. It is often found under tufts of grass growing with sphagnum moss* Lycopodium carolinianum *and the fern* Thelypteris confluens *in soak areas. It also grows on roadside banks where water trickles down. The red leaves have tiny glandular hairs round the edge and exude a sticky fluid which attracts insects. An insect stuck to the fluid is engulfed by the leaf and, after being partly dissolved, is absorbed by the plant. The glistening of the sticky fluid gives the plant its common name.*

## Tridactyle tricuspis

(specially protected plant)                                    ORCHIDACEÆ

*This orchid has a stem which is covered with the bases of the leaves. These strap-like leaves are arranged in two rows. The inflorescences grow from the stem below the leaves and the flowers are a creamy white. The specimen illustrated was growing on a rock under musasa trees in the Juliasdale area but the plant may also be epiphytic and the fleshy white aerial roots spread a considerable distance away from the plant.*

LAMIACEÆ

### Plectranthus hereroensis
(2m)

### Plectranthus zatarhendi
(1m)

### Aeollanthus buchnerianus
(30cm)

*Most of the plants of this family are aromatic and often have four-sided stems.* Plectranthus hereroensis *grows along the cliff edge from the Honde viewpoint right through to the Ringing Rocks of Chingamwe Estate. It is also found at World's View.* Plectranthus zatarhendi *has fleshy leaves and hairy stems and tends to grow in the shelter of rocks and boulders at high altitudes.* Aeollanthus buchnerianus, *unlike the shrubby plectranthus, is only about 30cm tall and often grows in cracks in the sheet rock of granite domes.*

# Aloe myriacantha

grass aloe  (50cm)  (specially protected plant)                    ALOEACEÆ

*In Zimbabwe,* Aloe myriacantha *is found only in the Eastern Highlands, but it is widespread throughout south and east Africa in similar habitats. Because of its size and very pale colour, this flower is often overlooked. It is usually found over 2000m growing in the open grasslands on mountains such as Chera, Rukotso, Mangua and Nyangani. It is resistant to fire as these areas get burnt during most years. The flowering time is between February and April.*

## *Scadoxus multiflorus*

(specially protected plant)  (30cm)                    AMARYLLIDACEÆ

*Found growing near a stream on the edge of the forest near the village of Buwu on the Honde path. The plant grows up to 30cm high and has leaves very similar to the* Scadoxus pole-evansii *illustrated on page 37.*

*The inflorescence is spherical and the delicate red flowers have protruding stamens and styles. Like others of this genus this plant sets berry-like fruit which ripen to a bright orange.*

ASTERACEAE

*There are many yellow-flowered Asteraceae that are superficially similar — in bloom at the same time. The five illustrated here are all from the grasslands of the Odzi basin. Because the grass is tall the flowers have long stems. Whole fields of* Helichrysum odoratissimum *make it conspicuous throughout the late summer.* Schistostephium artemisiifolium *lasts well in water and is being grown commercially for export.*

① *Helichrysum nudifolium*
  (1m)
② *Helichrysum umbraculigerum*
  (80cm)
③ *Nidorella auriculata*
  (50cm)
④ *Helichrysum odoratissimum*
  (40cm)
⑤ *Schistostephium artemisiifolium*
  (60cm)

①        ②        ③                    ④            ⑤

# April
## — the everlasting flowers

## Leonotis mollissima
lion's tail, nyamuchena  (1,5m)  LAMIACEÆ

## Anisopappus kirkii
(1m)    ASTERACEÆ

## Lantana sp.
(1m)   VERBENACEÆ

## Sparrmannia ricinocarpa
(1m)    TILIACEÆ

*These shrubs and those on the facing page were all found growing in the Nyakupinga valley. Now that the rains have eased, the warm sunlight has brought the summer growth into bloom.* Leonotis mollissima *may be up to 1,5 metres in height and even after frost has browned the flowers the plant is most conspicuous.*

Anisopappus kirkii *is a yellow daisy which may also be up to 1,5 metres high and is well worth a place in any garden.*

## Dombeya burgessiae
(3m)   STERCULIACEÆ

## Acrocephalus chirindensis
(80cm)   LAMIACEÆ

## Pavonia columella
(1m)   MALVACEÆ

## Hibiscus meeusei
(2m)   MALVACEÆ

*Dombeyas, which are known as wild pears, occur throughout Zimbabwe. This species grows in the medium to high altitude. The flowers may be white or pale pink.*

*Pavonia columella* and Hibiscus meeusei *are both of the Malvaceae. The* Pavonia *grows in thickets on forest edges, while the* Hibiscus *is found mainly in disturbed ground such as roadsides and disused lands.* Acrocephalus chirindensis *has an unusual flower head, which looks like a small dark purple-blue cone.*

## *Vernonia calvoana* subsp. *meridionalis*
(2m)   ASTERACEÆ

## *Vernonia karaguensis*
(1m)   ASTERACEÆ

*This is a very well represented genus of plants ranging from species only 20 or 30 centi-metres in height to shrubs such as* Vernonia myriantha *which may reach 4 metres in height. Most vernonia have a short flowering period and the fluffy white seeds often remain on the plant for longer than the flowers.*

Vernonia calvoana *flowers for longer than most of the family and it is a most decorative shrub.*

## Clematis brachiata

traveller's joy   RANUNCULACEÆ

*Sprawling over shrubs and trees this climber makes a wonderful sight in the lower altitude areas of Nyanga and Juliasdale.*

*The strong stems have no tendrils but are supported by the twining petioles. The flowers have no petals but four showy creamy-white sepals surrounding a powder-puff of radiating stamens. Like all this genus, the fruit is made up of feathery styles which remain on the plant for a long time. Because of this, it is sometimes known as 'old man's beard'.*

ASTERACEÆ

① *Helichrysum nitens*
  (40cm)
② *Helichrysum sulphureo-fuscum*
  (50cm)
③ *Helichrysum herbaceum*
  (25cm)
④ *Helichrysum setosum*
  (1m)
⑤ *Helichrysum goetzeanum*
  (1m)

# *Helichrysum adenocarpum*

pink everlasting    (30cm)            (SPECIALLY  PROTECTED  PLANT)                    ASTERACEÆ

This helichrysum has a basal rosette of woolly silver-grey leaves from which the flower stems grow. The leaves growing up the stem are sometimes close enough to give the stems themselves a woolly appearance. The involucral bracts surrounding the golden-yellow florets may vary in colour from crimson to pink or even white. These plants grow in the high, wet areas of the escarpment and the Downs in the open grass. They are specially protected plants within the Nyanga Intensive Conservation Area.

# CRASSULACEÆ

① *Crassula nodulosa*
(80cm)

② *Crassula swaziensis*
(20cm)

③ *Crassula sarcocaulis*
(50cm)

④ *Crassula vaginata*
(30cm)

⑤ *Crassula alticola*
(10cm)

These species of crassula are succulent and are often found in the most inhospitable places, like cracks in bare granite sheets, or amongst Aloe inyangensis, on the edge of the sheet rocks near the summit of Nyangani.

The flowers of C. vaginata *are small and white, and very insignificant, but when they fade, the cinnamon-red of the inflorescence is eye-catching.*

C. swaziensis *forms large colonies, often at very high altitudes.*

C. sarcocaulis, *growing in cracks or on ledges, has the bonsai appearance of a small tree, particularly as the 'trunk' and 'branches' are often covered with lichen.*

C. alticola *is the most delicate of the group and may be found trailing near water.*

④

①

②

⑤

③

# Viola abyssinica
(30cm)   VIOLACEÆ

# Selaginella abyssinica
(10cm)   SELAGINELLACEÆ

# Isachne mauritiana
(20cm)   POACEÆ

Viola abyssinica, *the wild violet, is a creeping or trailing perennial that roots at nodes. It pushes its way through surrounding vegetation, or may form a dense carpet in clearings in the forest, or along shady stream banks. The flowers may be almost white to a bluish-violet.*

Selaginella abyssinica *is a very slender semi-prostrate plant. It grows on wet stream banks in the dappled shade of the forests. It is so fine that the lacy layers appear almost translucent.*

Isachne mauritiana *is a delicate forest grass that may form stands of twenty or more square metres. During winter it dies down.*

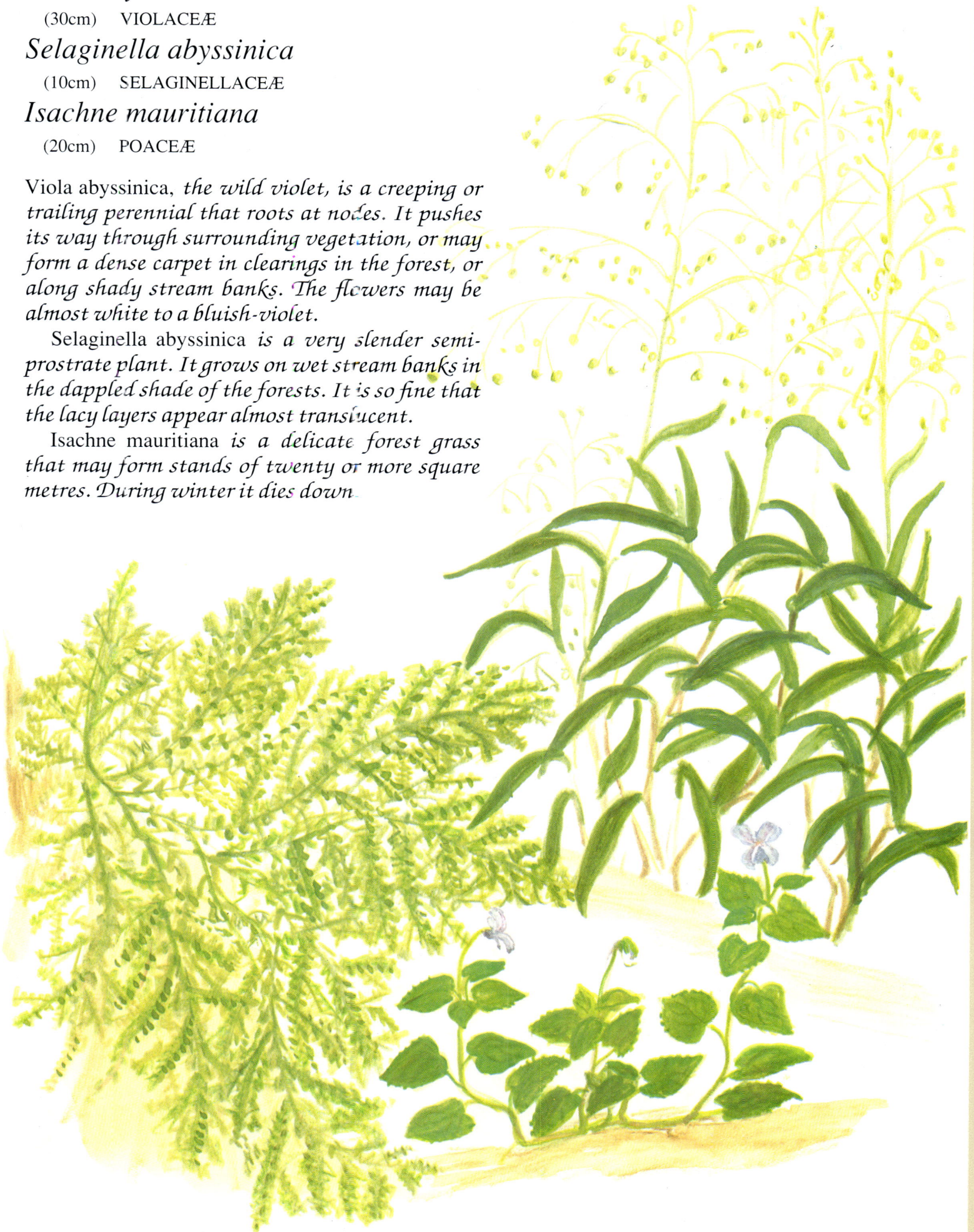

## Thunbergia alata

black-eyed susan ACANTHACEÆ

Occurring throughout the Eastern Districts
it grows from a perennial rootstock and is
often seen sprawling over bushes and
shrubs at the roadside.

## Cyphostemma montanum

VITACEÆ

Found in the wet areas; often growing over
shrubs on the edge of the forest or upon river
bank vegetation.

## Stephania abyssinica

MENISPERMACEÆ

With its insignificant flowers is most
interesting because of its decorative
peltate leaves. As this plant is host to a
fruit-piercing moth it is often eradicated
by using herbicides.

## Rumex sagittatus

climbing sorrel POLYGONACEÆ

This is related to the coral creeper and at
this time of the year makes a great splash of
colour as it sprawls over shrubs and grasses.

③

④

# Grasses

*April is the time of the year
when the grass seeds.*

③ *Loudetia simplex*
④ *Axonopus affinis*
⑤ *Melinis repens*
⑥ *Hyparrhenia filipendula*
① *Panicum monticola*
⑦ *Melinis minutiflora*
② *Monocymbium
ceresiiforme*
⑧ *Cymbopogon nardus*
⑨ *Themeda triandra*

# May

## – looking at ferns

# Introduction to ferns

Ferns and allied plants such as marattias, selaginellas and lycopodiums are covered by the scientific name Pteridophyta.

They do not flower and set seeds, but instead produce spores which germinate into tiny plants known as prothalli or gametophytes. It is at this stage that fertilization takes place and the new plant called a sporophyte begins to grow.

Because of the high rainfall and humidity, Nyanga is ideal for Pteridophyta. The greatest variety and concentration is in the wet forest areas of the escarpment from the Mtarazi Falls to the eastern slopes of Nyangani and the Kairezi River. The ferns of the forest are often epiphytic, sometimes lithophytic and many are rare.

Most ferns carry sporangia containing spores on the back of the fronds. Identification of ferns is often based on the position and pattern of the sporangia.

① *Dryopteris inaequalis* is a large fern with softly arching fronds up to 1,7m long. It grows on the forest floor and near streams. Shown here is one pinna or division of the frond.

② *Pellaea calomelanos* var. swynnertoniana
About 40cm tall. This is a very robust variety of Pellaea calomelanos *and is found only in a few localities. It grows in partial shade.*

③ *Pleopeltis excavata*

④ *Loxogramme lanceolata*. Both have simple fronds and are epiphytic.

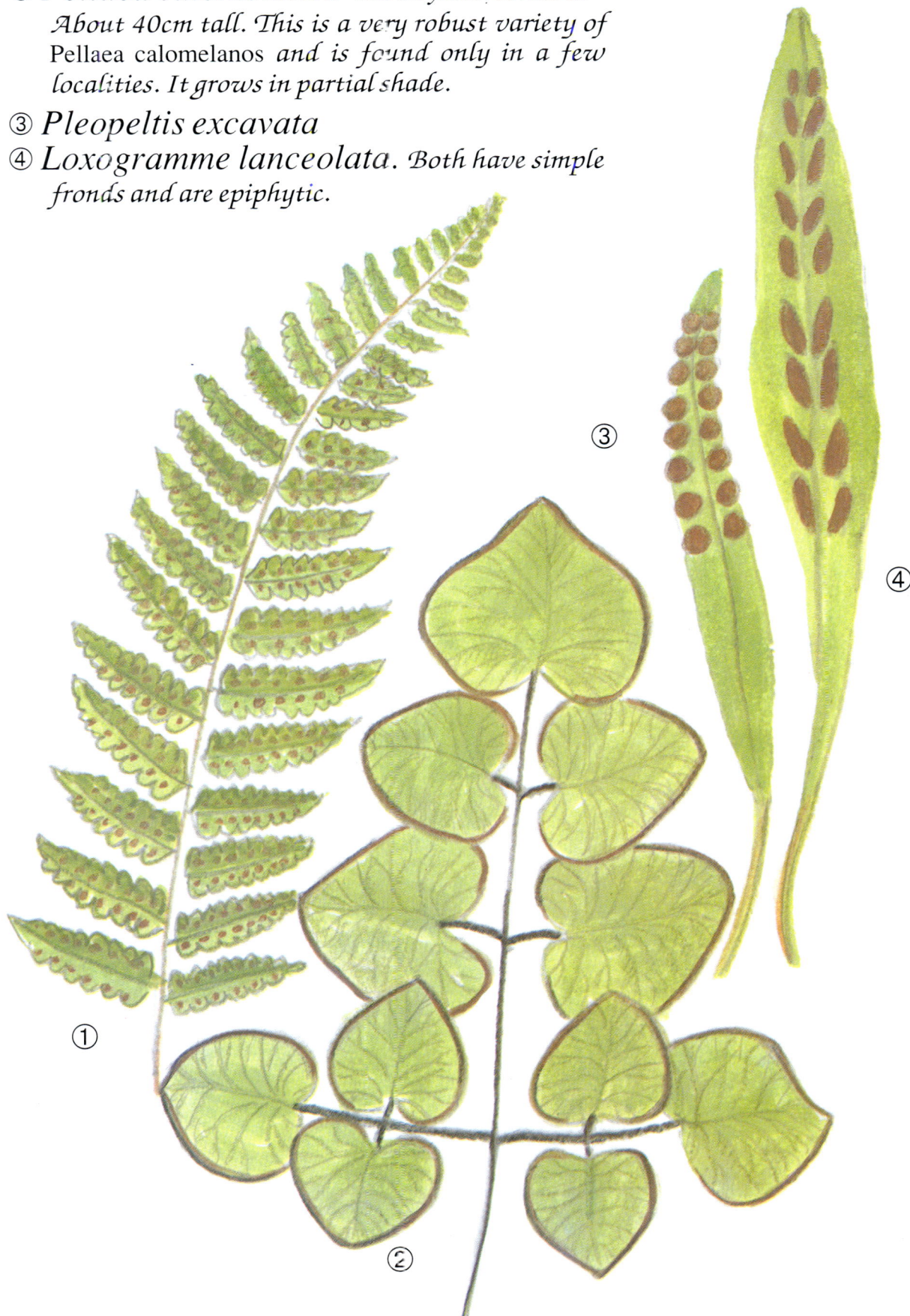

① ② ③ ④ ⑤ ⑥ ⑦

*Illustrated here are some of the aspleniums that grow mainly in the wet forests:*

① *Asplenium hypomelas*
② *Asplenium protensum*
③ *Asplenium theciferum*
④ *Asplenium rutifolium*
⑤ *Asplenium lobatum* var. *pseudoabyssinicum*
⑥ *Asplenium sandersonii*
⑦ *Asplenium anisophyllum*
⑧ *Asplenium friesiorum*
⑨ *Asplenium aethiopicum:* Widespread throughout Nyanga, the length of the fronds may vary from 15cm to over a metre in the high rainfall areas.

Another fern that grows throughout the area is Pteridium aquilinum *or bracken.* The specific name translates from Latin as 'like an eagle'. This is a pioneer plant and will often follow lichen and moss in disturbed areas.

⑧

⑨

## *Elaphoglossum aubertii*          *Blechnum attenuatum*

*Instead of sporangia on all fronds the more primitive ferns sometimes have fertile fronds that are unlike the sterile ones. The royal fern,* Osmunda regalis *(not illustrated), has a 'crown' of fertile pinnae.*

Elaphoglossum aubertii *has a fertile lamina that is spade-shaped and entirely covered by sporangia on one side. It grows on rocks or as a low-level epiphyte in the forest.*

Blechnum attenuatum *is a common fern of the wet areas. It often grows in roadside ditches. The fertile frond has much narrower pinnae than the other fronds.*

Some ferns also reproduce vegetatively:

Arthropteris monocarpa *has rhizomes that are widely creeping and new fronds arise from these. This fern is often epiphytic.*

Nephrolepis undulata *(sword fern) forms tubers up to 1,5cm long often at the end of long thin stolons. New plants grow from these stolons.*

Asplenium sandersonii, *which grows as an epiphyte or lithophyte in the deep shade, has proliferating buds at the tip of the frond so that it 'walks'.*

Tectaria gemmifera *has adventitious buds called gemmae which appear on the upper surface of the frond which will produce tiny fronds and when they drop off will root. This is also a forest fern.*

The new fronds of ferns are usually curled up and will unroll as the frond develops.

Three stages of the unfurling of the frond of Gleichenia umbraculifera *are shown here. This fern, often growing with* Dicranopteris linearis *will form dense stands on river banks or near rocks on the edge of the forest.*

Some ferns have simple undivided fronds like those of Vittaria isoetifolia *which is epiphytic and grows in the deep shade. It is tufted, sessile (without stalk), coriaceous (leathery), pendulous and dark green.*

Some ferns are finely divided like this pinna of Cheilanthes multifida *which grows in the open grassland.*

# Cyathea dregei

tree fern, chasenga

The stipes (stems of fronds) of ferns arise from a rhizome which is usually horizontal to the surface on which the plant grows. Sometimes the rhizome is vertical and forms a trunk called a caudex. Tree ferns may have a caudex up to five metres high.

There are four species of tree ferns in the Nyanga area and they are all specially protected plants:

Cyathea dregei, the common tree fern grows throughout both national parks, often on the banks of rivers and streams.

Cyathea capensis grows in the forest. The caudex is more slender than that of dregei.

Cyathea thomsonii is very like C. capensis but usually smaller and has pale brown hairs on the undersurface of the fronds.

Cyathea manniana, the 'thorny tree fern', is very slender and grows in the deep forest.

## Pellaea doniana              Arthropteris orientalis

*Although about sixty per cent of the species of ferns collected occur in the wet forest and escarpment areas, the* brachystegia *woodlands also have very beautiful ferns. These are often adapted to withstand periods of drought so may die down during the dry season or may fold up to prevent transpiration. Illustrated below are two of the ferns from such areas:*

Pellaea doniana *which grows on the ground in dry woodlands. It is not found much above 1650m.*

Arthropteris orientalis *grows in large colonies under musasa trees and between boulders. It is a tougher fern than* A. monocarpa *which is shown on page 91.*

# June
*– aloes ablaze*

## *Protea angolensis* var. *divaricata*

northern protea, chinhendere (3m)          PROTEACEAE

*Found in the open grassland around Nyanga village, this protea is a small tree reaching 3m in height. The flowers are about 10cm in diameter with green, white or even pink bracts. These plants seem to be able to withstand fire as almost every year this area is burnt.*

*A second variety, var. angolensis, is a sub-shrub that grows on the hills on the way to Troutbeck, often under dwarf musasas. Its new leaves form a rosette of bright red which is more eye-catching than the flower itself.*

## Erica simii (= Philippia simii)

philippia  (8m)

There are a number of species of Erica in the Nyanga area. They occur from the granite country right up to the beacon top of Nyangani. Some species may become small trees, while on rocky mountain tops some may cling close to the ground like an alpine plant. When in bloom they all shed a cloud of pollen.

## Erica johnstoniana

pink heath  (1m)

grows mainly above 2000m and is about a metre tall. The flowers are like little blocks in shape.

## Erica whyteana

(15cm)

grows in the wet soak areas where the streams that feed the Pungwe rise. The colour of the flowers may be from a pale pink to a bright cerise.

# *Aloe arborescens*

bush aloe, chikohwa  (3–4m)
ALOEACEÆ

*It is found throughout the Eastern Highlands, often in ancient ruins or on cliff faces such as those at Mtarazi Falls.*

SPECIALLY PROTECTED PLANT

# Aloe greatheadii

spotted leaf aloe, chikohwa (1,7m)

### ALOEACEÆ
(specially protected plant)

# Aloe swynnertonii

swynnerton's aloe, chikohwa (1,5m)

*The leaves of* Aloe greatheadii *form a stemless basal rosette. The flowers are pale pink or sometimes orange with inflorescences up to 1,7m in height. This aloe grows in the grasslands below 1800m.*

   Aloe swynnertonii *grows throughout the Eastern Districts. It too is stemless, but with bright green leaves in the form of a rosette. These leaves are marked in white oblongs.*

## Dissotis princeps

royal dissotis, ruhororo (3m)          MELASTOMATACEÆ

*This is a shrub that grows throughout the high rainfall areas of Zimbabwe. It may reach up to three metres in height in favourable places. The individual flowers are about 5cm across and bloom in succession, so extending the flowering season to about three months. Even when not in bloom the occasional orange or red leaf will make this shrub noticeable in the ochre-coloured grass of the winter. Before the frost comes* D. princeps *and* D. canescens *are often in bloom together.*

## *Aloe cameronii* var. *bondana*

cameron's aloe   (2m)   specially protected plant                                      ALOEACEÆ

*One of the most beautiful aloes as even without flowers it is a lovely sight with its reddish-bronze leaves. It has a compact rosette of leaves and in sheltered positions it may develop a stem and branch to form clumps. This plant grows on rocky exposed slopes and summits and can be found from Inyangani to Chera and Rukotso, as well as the granite hills of Bonda.*

## Acacia abyssinica

nyanga flat-top, muunga  (15m)                    FABACEÆ

*A very beautiful tree which grows up to fifteen metres in height and occurs in stands in the granite areas. The bark of these trees is brown to almost black, which makes the strange shape of the branches even more noticeable. Young trees have a paler, papery bark which peels off in layers. Flowering time is October to November when little white powder-puffs are produced.*

## Faurea saligna

beechwood    (8m)                                    PROTEACEÆ

*This is a small tree of the protea family. The leaves are long, narrow and drooping. In autumn they turn a lovely red and in spring the new leaves are a delicate pink. The inflorescence is a fluffy looking spike of pale pink flowers with persistent styles. A very strong honey scent makes this tree attractive to all sorts of insects. Faureas grow mainly in the granite brachystegia areas of Juliasdale.*

Shrubs and creepers from the
Mtarazi Falls area:

① *Tephrosia grandibracteata*
   FABACEÆ
② *Buddleja salviifolia*
   LOGANIACEÆ
③ *Polygala virgata*
   POLYGALACEÆ
④ *Freylinia tropica*
   mupfupa
   SCROPHULARIACEÆ

⑤ *Plectranthus hereroensis*
   LAMIACEÆ
⑥ *Hemizygia teucriifolia*
   LAMIACEÆ

⑦ *Ipomoea involucrata*
   CONVOLVULACEÆ
⑧ *Vigna gazensis*
   FABACEÆ
⑨ *Tetradenia riparia*
   ginger bush
   LAMIACEÆ

July

– burning of firebreaks

## Walafrida goetzei

(40cm)          SCROPHULARIACEÆ

Walafrida goetzei *grows in the Pungwe area. It is not as spectacular as the Selago but it is very beautiful with narrow heath-like leaves and branched inflorescences with a mass of tiny mauve flowers.*

## Selago thyrsoidea var. *austrorhodesiaca*

nyanga selago (40cm)     SCROPHULARIACEÆ

Selago thyrsoidea *belongs to same family as the Walafrida and grows in the Troutbeck area and the Nyanga Downs. It is a bushy perennial and may spread over as much as a metre when in bloom. One of the most beautiful flowers of Nyanga with its tiny mauve flowers forming dense trusses.*

## Aloe pretoriensis

chikohwa  (1,5m)                    ALOEACEÆ

This aloe grows throughout the Eastern Highlands. It is a specially protected plant and is usually found growing near rocks surrounded by low shrubs or small trees which afford it some protection from fire. It has a rosette of pale greyish-green leaves and is supported by a short stem often covered by dead leaves. The inflorescence is branched and each branch forms a raceme which may be up to 30cm long with pink to orange flowers which are covered with a distinct bloom.

## *Polystachya hollandii*

(20cm)  specially protected plant                    ORCHIDACEÆ

*A delicately perfumed orchid found growing in the forests near Mtarazi Falls. Although originally found in July, subsequent years have shown that flowering may be as early as March.*

*This orchid has slender pseudobulbs and strap-like leaves about 18cm long, that might well be mistaken for the fern Vittaria isoetifolia. The flowers are borne on thread-like stalks. As in other species of Polystachya, the lip is uppermost, so the ovary is not twisted. Because of the very high rainfall and mist, the forests of the area contain plants not found in many other places. The trees and rocks are covered by moss and ferns which protect the roots of the orchids that abound.*

## Clematopsis villosa

shock-headed peter  (1m)                    RANUNCULACEÆ

*Throughout the brachystegia woodlands are the upright silky mops of the* Clematopsis villosa *seed heads. Each seed has a 'tail' made up of silky hairs which enable seed dispersal. (See page 30.)*

## Sutera carvalhoi

(1m)                          SCROPHULARIACEÆ

Sutera carvalhoi *grows on rocky hillsides often supported by surrounding vegetation. It is a perennial over a metre in height. At this time of year, when so little is in bloom, the creamy-white flowers with orange-brown throats are very noticeable. They are often found in the same habitat as* Lantana sp.

*This plant is well worth a place in the garden and will grow easily either from a seed or from a cutting.*

# Introduction to mosses

Mosses, liverworts and hornworts are scientifically classified as Bryophytes. *Like ferns and their allies they produce spores but are much simpler plants as they lack conducting and supporting tissue.*

Bryophytes *depend on water to reproduce as the sperm 'swims' to the ovum. This ovum then grows into a spore-bearing plant which remains attached to the parent. A slender stem called a seta supports the capsule which, when ripe, sheds its cap; then the lid and the dust-like spore is dispersed.*

*There are many different mosses and liverworts: three pebbles collected in the bed of a stream near the Honde path yielded eight different mosses and one liverwort.*

Here are just a few mosses, some of
which are used by florists
and nurserymen:

① *Polytrichum commune*
   star moss
② *Leptodontium longicolle*
   florists' moss
③ *Funaria spathulata*
④ *Rhodobryum* sp.
⑤ *Campylopus procerus*
   thick moss
⑥ *Plagiochila divergens*

① ② ③ ④ ⑤ ⑥

## Lichens

*A lichen is made up by the combination of a unicellular alga and a fungus living in a symbiotic relationship. The alga makes food for them both by photosynthesis, while the fungus protects the alga and draws water from the air. Because of this combined effort a lichen can survive where no other plant can. They grow on bare rocks, on trees and on the ground, and are some of the most important pioneer plants. Many road embankments in the Troutbeck area have patches of grey lichen and, throughout Nyanga, trees are draped with grey-green 'old man's beard'.*

*Lichen reproduces vegetatively, by each partner multiplying in its usual way, or by producing reproductive bodies called soredia, which is a substance like a grey dust. The cup-like structures seen at certain times of the year are the fruit-body of the fungus.*

*Lichens are very slow growing and very sensitive to industrial pollution. In parts of industrial Europe and North America, lichens have been almost entirely destroyed.*

## Bracket fungi

The fruiting body of these fungi consists of a crust with a spore-bearing layer attached. The arrangement of this layer depends on the species. Bracket fungi are part of Nature's decomposition of wood.

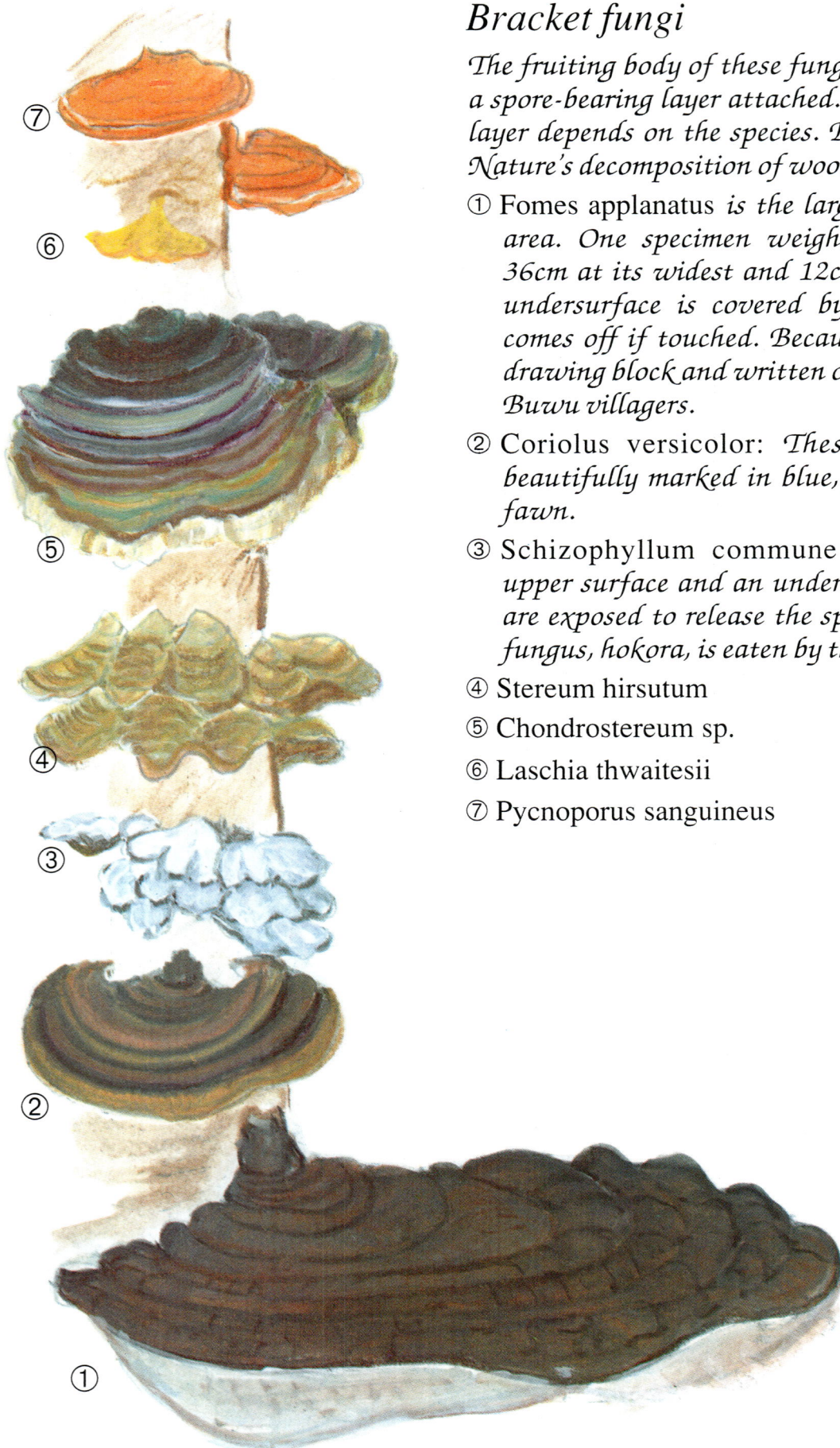

① Fomes applanatus *is the largest species found in our area. One specimen weighed 2,8kg and measured 36cm at its widest and 12cm thick at the base. The undersurface is covered by a white bloom which comes off if touched. Because of this it is used as a drawing block and written on to pass messages by the Buwu villagers.*

② Coriolus versicolor: *These are fan-shaped and beautifully marked in blue, grey, brown and golden fawn.*

③ Schizophyllum commune *has an almost hairy upper surface and an undersurface with gills which are exposed to release the spore in dry weather. This fungus, hokora, is eaten by the local people.*

④ Stereum hirsutum

⑤ Chondrostereum sp.

⑥ Laschia thwaitesii

⑦ Pycnoporus sanguineus

# August
## – *musasa time*

## *Brachystegia spiciformis* (musasa)

FABACEÆ

*A beautiful deciduous tree that can grow up to 15 metres in height. The bark is grey and rough. It has short spikes of insignificant, but sweetly scented white flowers. In late August and early October there is a spring flush of new leaves which may be a delicate pale green, red, bronze or Indian yellow. The hills glow with colour.*

*Two thousand and sixty metres is the approximate upper altitude limit for musasa. Between 1800m and this height, particularly on north-west facing slopes, the trees are dwarfed, often only two metres in height with crowns flattened and trunks and branches gnarled. They grow in groups with bare or sparsely covered ground between.*

# Hypericum revolutum

curry bush, ruhurukuru  (3m)                                        CLUSIACEÆ

Hypericum revolutum *is a shrubby St. John's wort. It is easy to recognize by its distinct curry smell. Blooms appear at intervals throughout the year and with the early rains it becomes covered with buds.*

*The flowers are 4 to 5cm in diameter and a bright yellow with the centre filled with yellow stamens.*

*This plant grows from about 1800m and right up to the summit of Nyangani. In the wet misty conditions of the escarpment* Hypericum revolutum *may be a small tree and may cover whole hillsides. Under these trees conditions are ideal for the moss* Leptodontium longicolle *which often completely carpets the ground.*

# Hypericum roeperianum

St. John's wort (1,5m)                                                 CLUSIACEÆ

*Large-leaved St. John's wort which grows along the edges of the forests and streams in areas below 1800m. It is altogether a much more substantial shrub than* Hypericum revolutum *as it has larger leaves and the flowers are less fragile. If a leaf is held up to the light tiny transparent marks will be seen. These are oil glands and if leaves and a few flowers are placed in a glass jar and covered with oil, after about two weeks of sunlight, the oil will turn a rich, ruby red. This is a healing balm much used by herbalists the world over and was carried by the Crusaders to mend their wounds: hence the name St. John's wort. The flowers are about 5cm across and are sought after by bees and other insects.*

# Erythrina lysistemon

eastern district's lucky bean tree, musodzo (7m)                    FABACEÆ

*The scarlet flowers of this tree are a great splash of colour in a dry and often blackened landscape. Growing to a height of 6 to 7 metres it has dark grey smooth bark. The flowers are produced in short dense heads of about 8cm length on long bare stalks. The slender black seed pods are up to 15cm long and, inside, are bright orange to red 'lucky beans'.*

## Smilax anceps

scrambler, garuwa    SMILACACEÆ

*It was like finding a tiger with a ribbon around its neck to find a smilax in bloom. This vicious creeper, with paired tendrils and hooked thorns, fortunately, only grows below 1800m. Walking through a thicket of smilax is almost impossible.*

*The female plant, after flowering, sets beautiful grape-like purple berries covered with a soft bloom. The stem is split and used to bind and decorate baskets.*

## Rubus rigidus

bramble, marugato    ROSACEÆ

*The bramble with the black berries is* Rubus rigidus, *while the sweeter, bright orange berry is* Rubus pinnatus. *The two species are often intertwined and in areas of disturbed ground may form a thick tangle. They grow throughout the Nyanga area.*

*Other than smilax and brambles, there are certain species of* Protasparagus *and* Acacias *that are armed with thorns. At lower altitudes, disused fields sometimes have patches of stud thorn (*Dicerocaryum senecicides), *but on the whole there are few thorny plants, so walking is relatively easy.*

## Halleria lucida

tree fuchsia (2,5m)                                        SCROPHULARIACEÆ

*It is often the fallen flowers on a path in the forest that attract attention to this small tree as the shiny bright green leaves almost hide the flowers. The flowers are brick-red and orange and hang down in clusters from twigs and branches. A halleria in bloom will be alive with birds. The fruit which is oval in shape, turns black when ripe and is edible, but tends to make the mouth dry. It is found mainly in thickets at the forest edge or along stream banks.*

## Senecio tamoides

scrambler  ASTERACEÆ

*Great mounds of brilliant yellow daisies cover trees and shrubs along the edge of wooded areas throughout the district.*

## Senecio deltoideus

canary creeper (scrambler)  ASTERACEÆ

*Has a soft-leaf with a serrated edge, which may turn bright red or purple in the dry season. The flower heads are not as densely packed as in Senecio tamoides, but are most attractive.*

## Buddleja auriculata

eared buddleja, chepambati   (3m)                                    LOGANIACEÆ

*The upper surface of the leaves are glossy which makes it easy to distinguish from the dull-leaved* Buddleja salviifolia. *Often found near ancient ruins, its flowers may be pink, mauve, cream or orange.*

## Buddleja salviifolia

butterfly bush, chepambati  (4m) LOGANIACEÆ

*Grows throughout the Nyanga area and may be tall enough to be called a tree. The leaves are often eaten by insects. Flowers vary from white to the deep mauve illustrated here.*

# September
## – the phoenix flowers

# Pteridium aquilinum

bracken    PTERIDOPHYTA

# Knowltonia transvaalensis

white anemone  (75cm)  RANUNCULACEÆ

*Arising out of the ashes of the burnt areas come first the shoots of bracken with tiny curled fists slowly unfurling. Next comes the green of the grass and the new leaves of* Senecio latifolius.

*The early flowering plants are those with perennial rootstocks which are stimulated by fire. Many thrust up flower heads before producing leaves.*

*The delicate white flowers of* Knowltonia transvaalensis *are about 4cm across with many stamens clustered around the carpels. It is found growing in rocky areas along the escarpment.*

# Trichodesma physaloides

bells of St. Mary's or chocolate bells  (60cm)
BORAGINACEÆ

The flowers of Trichodesma physaloides make a lovely show throughout the area except the highest and wettest parts along the edge of the escarpment.

Around Nyanga village in an area burnt almost every year there are great patches of these flowers. The plant grows to a height of 60cm and has dark browny-red stems with pointed leaves up to 6cm long. The white bell-shaped flowers hang down and are most attractive with the brown edge to each petal. The thick perennial root is used to treat skin complaints.

A second member of this genus, Trichodesma ambacense, which has pale blue flowers instead of white, grows in the Cumberland valley area.

# Cyathea dregei

tree fern  (5m)

*Cut down by frost every winter, the old fronds of the common tree fern, Cyathea dregei  have now dropped and the new fronds, like shepherds' crooks covered with silky brown hairs, are just starting to uncurl. Set at regular intervals around the crown of the fibrous trunk, the fronds grow very rapidly now that the weather has warmed. Porcupines relish these new fronds and may spend night after night gnawing the caudex (trunk) of the fern until it falls and the feast can begin.*

By the middle of the month, if there has been rain, many more perennials come into bloom. These plants produce leaves first and may continue to flower all summer.

ASTERACEÆ

① *Athrixia rosmarinifolia*, or manica daisy is a bushy perennial that may grow up to a metre in height. It is usually found in thickets on mountain slopes.

LAMIACEÆ

② *Hemizygia teucriifolia*, or mountain sage, is a compact perennial (up to 30cm high) with showy pink to purple bracts that remain long after the small flowers have dropped. The aromatic smell of this plant makes it easy to recognize.

SCROPHULARIACEÆ

③ *Graderia scabra*, known as pink groundbells, grows above 1800m in the open grasslands. Up to 20cm high, both stems and leaves are hairy and rough. The flowers are about 3cm long and may be bright pink to mauve.

SCROPHULARIACEÆ

④ *Cycnium adonense*, the ink plant, at about 12cm tall with white flowers, gets its common name from the fact that it will turn a dark purple-black if damaged. It is partly parasitic, attaching itself to the roots of its host.

RUBIACEÆ

⑤ *Pentanisia sykesii* grows to a height of 20cm, has clusters of bright blue flowers and is in bloom throughout the summer.

① *Dolichos kilimandscharicus*
wild lupin (75cm)

② *Indigofera hilaris*
(20cm)

③ *Rhynchosia monophylla*
fire pea

④ *Lotus namulensis*
(30cm)

*These flowers all belong to Papilionoideae, a sub-family of Fabaceae (= Leguminosae). They have perennial rootstocks and flower with the first rains of the season.*

*The most beautiful is* Dolichos kilimandscharicus *or wild lupin which grows to about 50cm from a very swollen rootstock. The leaves only appear as the flowers begin to set pods.*

Indigofera hilaris *is a bright pink and a single plant spreads over a large area. If the flowers come out before the leaves, as happens if there is early rain, it forms a wonderful splash of colour.*

*The luminous* Rhynchosia monophylla *or fire pea and the white* Lotus namulensis *were collected in the Pungwe area.*

① *Senecio latifolius*
ragwort, chezadzamutiro
(75cm)

② *Helichrysum pilosellum*
(30cm)

③ *Berkheya zeyheri*
sun daisy   (40cm)

④ *Gnidia kraussiana*
yellow heads   (30cm)

Senecio latifolius *is an erect plant that has an annual flower stem rising from a perennial root. The poison from this plant is cumulative and every year causes cattle losses. Another senecio,* Senecio striatifolius, *which is taller and with larger flowers, grows on open exposed mountain slopes such as Nyangani and Rukotso.*

Helichrysum pilosellum *has a white felting to the undersurface of its quilted leaves and its flower stems. It is often found growing in the tender new grass with the yellow single-stemmed* H. chasei. *At this time of year there are many yellow daisies in bloom.* Berkheya zeyheri *is easy to recognize as it has a fringe of fine bracts below the composite head.*

Gnidia kraussiana *is a plant with reddish stems and narrow leaves. The round inflorescences are up to 4cm across and are densely packed with small bright yellow flowers with tiny petals and marked sepals.*

## Herschelianthe baurii

(20cm)          ORCHIDACEÆ

*The mountain grasslands of the Troutbeck and Connemara areas support many lovely flowers, some found only there because of the high altitude and the soils.* Herschelianthe baurii *is an orchid 15 to 30cm in height with the leaves appearing after the flowers. These flowers are usually bright blue but some may be purple-blue, pinkish or even almost white. The lip is deeply dissected so that it looks like a beard.*

Herschelianthe chimanimaniensis *is the only other species of this genus that grows in Zimbabwe.*

## LOBELIACEÆ

### Monopsis decipiens
(15cm)

### Lobelia erinus
(30cm)

### Lobelia goetzei
(30cm)

*Members of the lobelia family occur in many areas of Zimbabwe and some flower throughout the year. The most vivid is* Monopsis decipiens *which grows in great profusion in damp grassy places or in shallow pockets that retain moisture. Where fire has swept an area these tiny plants will come into flower at the same time making a carpet of blooms.*

Lobelia erinus *comes in many shades of blue often with a white throat. It is almost as spectacular as* Monopsis decipiens, *although the individual flowers are much smaller.*

Lobelia goetzei *is pale mauve to pink and often grows in the same areas as* L. erinus. *These plants are usually perennials but may flower in the first year. They are among the earliest of the spring flowers to come into bloom and in the short grass of the exposed mountain tops make a fine display.*

The pine trees, Pinus patula, *are in full flower and a cloud of pollen fills the air coating everything with a layer of yellow dust. It is easy to see how in the geological past pollen has been preserved within sedimentary rocks and in the peat.*

*The wattle trees,* Acacia mearnsii, *are also starting to flower. The tips of each branch catching the light with a yellow glow. Pity anyone suffering from hay-fever!*

*Both these trees are of great commercial importance to Zimbabwe. Originally from Mexico, the patula is the main softwood used both for construction timber and in pulp for the making of paper. The wattle tree, from Australia, yields tannin from the bark and the timber is used for pit props or as a general timber.*

*Unfortunately, both these species seed readily and considerable areas of Nyanga have been invaded. Efforts are made, particularly in the national parks, to eradicate these two trees, but it is a daunting task.*

# Cyrtanthus rhodesianus

fire lily (20cm) specially protected plant
AMARYLLIDACEÆ

The fire lily grows in the wet
soak areas of valley bottoms
and will often come into bloom
within a short while of fire remov-
ing the grass cover. A second species,
Cyrtanthus contractus, which is
very similar in appearance, but
with leaves that appear after the
flowers, occurs amongst the rocks
on hillslopes or near cliff edges. The
scarlet of these fire lilies against
the grey lichen-covered rocks of the
Mtarazi Falls is a study in contrast.

# Albuca kirkii
(30cm)  HYACINTHACEÆ

# Alepidea swynnertonii
(20cm)  APIACEÆ

# Vernonia hirsuta
(20cm)  ASTERACEÆ

# Tulbaghia friesii
wild garlic  (10cm)  ALLIACEÆ

# Harveya randii
(6cm)  SCROPHULARIACEÆ

*Along the eastern escarpment overlooking the Honde valley is an area of open mountain grassland known as Mangua. Because of the wind most of the spring flowers are low growing and come from perennial rootstock or are bulbous.*

*Albuca kirkii with its green and white petals is sometimes called a snake lily. The flowers push up through the burnt grass before the leaves appear.*

*The white star-shaped Alepidea swynnertonii can be recognized by the fine hairs like eyelashes along the edge of the flat leaves. It blooms throughout the summer.*

*Vernonia hirsuta is one of the many vernonias of the district and is about 30cm tall.*

*Harveya randii is parasitic on the roots of grass and is only 2 to 3cm high.*

*The little Tulbaghia friesii has a very strong garlic smell when the leaves are damaged. It often grows in shallow pockets in exposed sheet rock.*

## Cussonia spicata

mountain cabbage tree  (10m)

ARALIACEÆ

*It may grow up to 10 metres tall, but along the escarpment, is usually gnarled and stunted. The leaves form tufts on the end of the branches and the flowers are in thick spikes up to 15cm long and held up in bunches. Some very fine specimens of this tree may be seen in the Rhodes Nyanga National Park, on the way to the Experiment Station.*

## Widdringtonia nodiflora

mountain cedar  (7m)

specially protected plant

CUPRESSACEÆ

*A small, scrubby tree, from 4 to 6 metres in height, that grows along the edge of the escarpment. It is subject to frequent fires, and it is only where protection is afforded by rocks or cliffs, that trees of any stature remain.*

ERIOSPERMACEÆ

① *The yellow* Eriospermum cecilii *belongs to a family of its own related to the lilies. It flowers before it has leaves. (15cm)*

CARYOPHYLLACEÆ

② Silene burchellii *is a slender plant growing from a perennial root. The flowers are pale pink or cream and it can easily be recognized by its distinctive seed pods. (30cm)*

CAMPANULACEÆ

③ *Wahlenbergia undulata (30cm)*

ASTERACEÆ

④ *Grey-leaved* Vernonia natalensis *forms clumps and is very common throughout Nyanga. (30cm)*

PASSIFLORACEÆ

⑤ *The flat green leaves of* Basananthe sandersonii *are often found on roadside banks. The flower is most unexpected and the shiny seed pod out of all proportion. Related to passion fruit. (5cm)*

HYACINTHACEÆ

⑥ Ledebouria revoluta *has purple blotched leaves and flowers that are as beautiful as those of a grape hyacinth. (10cm)*

ANTHERICACEÆ

⑦ Chlorophytum pygmaeum *with its leathery leaves that fit neatly into one another. (30cm)*

## Stoebe vulgaris

hanya (2 m) ASTERACEÆ

*An ericoid shrub which grows in tangled stands throughout the area. It may be as much as two metres high and makes walking very difficult.*

*The flowers are small and spiky and form an inflorescence. The twigs are set at almost a right angle to the stems which gives the plant a most distinctive appearance.*

*A gall often infests this shrub and the little white woolly blobs can be mistaken for flower heads or seeds. When clearing takes place for cultivation, 'hanya' is cut at ground level. The plants are rolled one into another until a bundle, sometimes two metres high, is formed.*

## Euphorbia depauperata     Euphorbia citrina

(25cm)          EUPHORBIACEÆ          (1m)

*These two euphorbias were found at the Honde viewpoint.
E. citrina has only recently been named in spite of being very
common and striking in the Mtarazi area. The milky latex of
euphorbias is sometimes used medicinally but may cause skin
irritation and temporary blindness if it gets in the eyes.*

# October

*– sunshine*

## Helichrysum splendidum

mapete (1m) ASTERACEÆ

*The grey-leaved* Helichrysum splendidum *is in bloom. The clusters of small very bright yellow everlasting flowers cover the bush. This helichrysum grows throughout Nyanga. In some areas, whole valleys or hillsides may be clothed with this plant to the exclusion of most else, except bracken, or perhaps* Blaeria friesii. *The aromatic smell which clings to one's clothes is part of the charm of the mountains.*

## Helichrysum swynnertonii

(7cm) ASTERACEÆ

*Another everlasting,* Helichrysum swynnertonii, *is also in bloom. The plant has grey leaves and large flowers with shiny white bracts which surround a dome of bright yellow florets. This is one of the most beautiful of the helichrysums which grow in the granite soils of Juliasdale.*

## Triumfetta welwitschii

triumfetta (50cm)  TILIACEÆ

The roads from Rusape and from Mutare converge close to the Juliasdale business centre. The triangle between is a large tract of very broken country. Huge granite outcrops such as Manyoli and Susurumba rise out of boulder-clad hillslopes.

The sandy, coarse-grained soils of much of this area support plants not found in the more acid soils of other parts of Nyanga. One of the plants of the granites is Triumfetta welwitschii. This has yellow flowers with small petals and showy sepals. The flower buds and new leaves are covered with a brownish felt. It forms bright patches of colour on the grassy hillsides over a long period of time as the soft burr-like seed capsules are as decorative as the flowers.

## *Thunbergia lancifolia*

blue thunbergia (50cm) ACANTHACEÆ

Thunbergia lancifolia *is one of the first plants to appear after the burn, but it is only now that it has come into bloom. The flowers which are about 4cm across vary from a pale blue to the deep blue illustrated here. The yellow throats emphasize the lovely blue.*

*Thunbergia natalensis with pale violet-blue flowers grows in the shade close to the edges of the forest along the escarpment. Each flower only lasts a day but it makes a great show.*

*It is interesting to note, that in 1987, when the rains were very late, neither* Thunbergia lancifolia, *nor* T. natalensis, *flowered, despite the good rains that followed.*

① *Pelargonium luridum*        ututye  (1m)

flowers for a relatively short while. The flowers on tall slender stems stand up above the green grass varying in colour from cream to a dull pink. Both leaves and flowers are delicately perfumed.

② *Pelargonium graveolens*        (1m)

is a sweetly scented shrub-like plant that grows in the shelter of rocks in the Troutbeck area.

③ *Geranium nyassense*        geranium  (20cm)

A true geranium, varying from white to pale pink, and one of the plants that blooms throughout the year. It is often the odd vivid orange or red lacy leaf that catches the eye rather than the flowers.

①

②

③

*Hypoxis obtusa*            *Hypoxis angustifolia*            *Hypoxis pungwensis*

nyachinjo  (30cm)            yellow stars  (10cm)            (30cm)

Hypoxis obtusa *is found throughout the area and the green of the new leaves, which rise from the fleshy yellow rootstock, is one of the first signs of spring.*

*Hypoxis angustifolia, the little one, grows on exposed mountain slopes, often where there is only a thin soil cover.*

*Hypoxis pungwensis has very hairy leaves and flower stems. Although the flowers are no larger than those of* H. obtusa, *the plant is generally heavier.*

# Pachycarpus concolor       Trachycalymma fimbriatum

ASCLEPIADACEAE    (milkweed)

The flowers are five-lobed and the stamens are united into a column in the centre. The colours are muted browns, yellows, greens or maroons, but often the combination of colours is startling.

Because of the geometric symmetry of the individual blooms, and the precise placing within the inflorescence, these flowers look remarkably like glass paper-weights. The fruit is an inflated ball, sometimes long and thin, sometimes almost round and covered with hairs. When these pods open, the seeds burst out and are carried away on tiny silken parachutes.

## *Boophane disticha*

tumbleweed (40cm)   AMARYLLIDACEÆ

Boophane disticha *grows mainly in the granite areas of Juliasdale. The neck of the large bulb is above the ground and from this emerges the bud. As it opens the florets spread out to form a round ball. As the flowers fade, the stalklets lengthen and become rigid, so forming a seed-head, which becomes detached from the plant and is rolled along by the wind. The leaves, arranged like a fan, only emerge after the seed head has blown away. The plant is very poisonous.*

# Crinum macowanii   river lily  (50cm)   AMARYLLIDACEÆ

The lilies of the river valleys. The Nyakupinga and the Odzi valleys have great groups of them in bloom at this time of the year. The long strap-like leaves have undulate edges and the thick peduncle comes out of the bulb next to the leaves. The flowers are trumpet-shaped, each 20cm long. The seeds, when ripe, germinate readily.

## Gazania krebsiana subsp. serrulata

gazania (10cm)   ASTERACEÆ

*A new batch of flowers have come out in the Ringing Rocks area. Some are low to the ground like the Gazania krebsiana, with its dark green leaves with white felted backs. With the rain, the hollows in the rocks have filled with water and mats of moss and grey-green selaginella have revived. The tufts of old man's beard (Usnea sp.), which go stiff and brittle in the dry season, are now soft again.*

## Lindernia pulchella

mole's spectacles (2cm)   SCROPHULARIACEÆ

*A tiny plant that also grows on the rafts of matted grass. The flowers rise from a rosette of leaves and colonies of these form bright patches of colour when in bloom.*

*Some lichens are sending up tiny little spore heads, some a flesh pink, while others are bright scarlet, like little toadstools.*

## Eulophia zeyheri

(8cm)   ORCHIDACEÆ

*The leaf-bearing shoot stands next to the flower stem, and often the leaves only appear after the flower. The leaves of many of the* Eulophia *species are pleated, as are both these illustrated here.*

Eulophia zeyheri, *also known as the banana orchid, because the buds resemble a bunch of tiny yellow bananas. Hundreds of these orchids come out at the same time in favourable areas on Claremont estate.*

## Eulophia streptopetala

(1m)   ORCHIDACEÆ

*Grows in the Juliasdale area. A very fine specimen was also found in the Nyakupinga valley. The stems are often over a metre long.*

## Scabiosa columbaria
DIPSACACEÆ

## Scilla nervosa
(20cm)   HYACINTHACEÆ

## Ledebouria sp.
(8cm)   HYACINTHACEÆ

## Vernonia galpinii
ASTERACEÆ

*Now that the grass is long, the flowers are often almost hidden.* Scabiosa columbaria, *with its long slender stem, is able to rise about the grass, but the others in this group tend to grow in open patches between tufts or near rocks.*

Scilla nervosa *has light green leaves with raised veins. This plant was found in the grasslands near Nyanga village.*

*The* Ledebouria sp. *is a much smaller plant with deep purple backing to the leaves.*

Vernonia galpinii *is of the Asteraceae family and its vivid cerise flowers are very beautiful.*

# Erythrina latissima

broad-leaved coral tree, musodzo    (6m)    FABACEÆ

*This tree is more widely distributed than* Erythrina lysistemon, *and many fine specimens can be seen in the Rhodes Nyanga National Park. The tree reaches up from 5 to 7 metres in height with branches that are stubby and covered with sharp hooked thorns. The large, leathery, trifoliate leaves, when young, are covered with a woolly felt, and may also have thorns. The flowers are a beautiful scarlet-red with inflorescences up to 15 centimetres in diameter.*

# Aloe maculata

chikohwa   ALOEACEÆ

*This aloe was found growing halfway up Mount Nyangani. There are eleven plants in this particular colony. They grow only here, and on the Downs beyond Troutbeck, where the altitude is above 2000 metres and dolerite overlays granite. The plant is without a stem and the spotted leaves are a dark, dull green, with the tips often withered and curled under. The inflorescence are about 60cm long with bright orange flowers 35 to 40cm in length. The sap of this plant is reputed to be a cure for wounds.*

# November
*— the start of the rains*

# Chlorophytum galpinii
(30cm)   ANTHERICACEÆ

# Otiophora inyangana
(25cm)   RUBIACEÆ

# Acalypha caperonioides
(12cm)   EUPHORBIACEÆ

The first flush of flowers is over, but there are still patches of colour. Illustrated here is Chlorophytum galpinii, a perennial which grows from a woody rhizome. The leaves are slightly pleated and the flowers white with a brown stripe down the petals. Only a few flowers are open at a time but the plant has a long flowering season.

Otiophora inyangana is a red-stemmed, most decorative, small shrub with pale mauve flowers which would be well worth growing in a garden.

The red Acalypha caperonioides is a curiosity, as male and female flowers are on separate plants and are quite different. The male plant is the one with the long cone-like flowers, and the female, the fluffy threads.

# *Androcymbium striatum*

african crocus  (20cm)   COLCHICACEÆ

*Androcymbium striatum* has a number of common names including 'little men in boats', 'pyjama flowers', 'Moses in the basket' and 'african crocus'. The small green flowers with bright yellow anthers are held by large green and white striped bracts. The leaves are keel-shaped and the entire plant only about 20cm high. There are large colonies of these flowers on either side of the road from London Store right through to Nyanga village. The triangle at the junction of the Rusape and Mutare roads has such a colony and is a very pleasing sight.

## Xerophyta equisetoides

vellozia, phewo   (50cm)   VELLOZIACEÆ

*Growing on the granite domes and rocky hillslopes, on fibrous mats of tangled roots, humus and dry selaginella, are the seemingly dry dead stems of these plants. Fire may burn some of the outer old leaf bases that make up these stems, but in spite of that, when the first real, good soaking rain falls, out come the fresh green leaves, then the most unlikely pale mauve flowers. All the plants in a colony will come into bloom at the same time but last only a few days, and will not flower again until the next year.*

# Aristea ecklonii
### (20cm)

# Aristea woodii
### (40cm)

IRIDACEÆ

The tall bright blue Aristea ecklonii grows in the forested areas along the escarpment. The flowers open in the early morning but by noon have closed to a twisted spiral.

The smaller Aristea woodii was found growing in the open near the summit of Mount Nyangani. The leaves are much shorter, a lighter green, and not as ribbed as those of A. ecklonii. Both these aristeas keep blooming until the end of February.

# Dierama formosum
### (1m)  specially protected plant  IRIDACEÆ

This dierama is a much darker colour than the one illustrated on page 57, and is neither as tall, nor as graceful in habit.

② ③ ① ④ ⑤ ⑥

① *Behnia reticulata*
② *Protasparagus africanus*
③ *Protasparagus virgatus*
④ *Protasparagus plumosus*
⑤ *Protasparagus setaceus*
⑥ *Myrsiphyllum asparagoides*

These flowers were all found growing in the Juliasdale area.

① *Plectranthus stenophyllus*
   LAMIACEÆ

② *Dolichos kilimandscharicus*
   wild lupin    FABACEÆ

③ *Vigna macrorhyncha*
   FABACEÆ

④ *Swertia welwitschii*
   (15cm)    GENTIANACEÆ

⑤ *Sebaea leiostyla*
   GENTIANACEÆ

⑥ *Salvia nilotica*
   LAMIACEÆ

⑦ *Crotalaria valida*
   FABACEÆ

These plants are Apiaceae *or* Umbelliferae*, and within this family are many of our herbs and vegetables, such as parsley, parsnips and carrots. The plants are both aromatic and have umbels of small greenish-white flowers.*

## Peucedanum nyassicum
   (2m)   APIACEÆ
*Grows in profusion in the Juliasdale area and has most decorative seed heads.*

## Peucedanum rhodesicum
   (1,5m)   APIACEÆ
*Grows at higher altitudes, often in exposed areas such as Mount Nyangani and Mangua.*

## Passerina montana

(2,5m)   THYMELAEACEÆ

This attractive shrub grows in some areas of Nyanga and yet is completely absent in others. It grows, for example, in the Nyakupinga valley, but not along the Pungwe scenic drive. The determining factor is not obvious. It grows around London Store and right up to the summit of Nyangani. It grows on the granites and dolerites of the mountains, but not along the escarpment. It grows in the wet areas, as well as the rain-shadow areas of Juliasdale.

   The plants on Nyangani are much more compact than those from the more sheltered areas, and the tiny bracts may be yellow, pink or the more common brick-red. At first glance the plant might be mistaken for an erica, but if in doubt, break off a twig and, if the bark peels off up to the stem, it is passerina.

## Haplocarpha thunbergii

(25cm)   ASTERACEÆ

*Groups of these bright yellow daisies are in bloom along the scenic drive and in the National Park.*

*The oval leaves have a white-felted undersurface, and the buds and flower stems are also coated.*

*Like almost all members of the Asteraceae, the flower head is, in fact, an inflorescence. It has small flowers called florets, packed together on a base, and these are surrounded by a circle of ray florets, which are the petals of the daisy.*

# December

*– a month of storms*

# *Aloe rhodesiana*                                                    *Aloe inyangensis*

chikohwa (25cm)                    ALOEACEÆ                    (35cm)

Aloe rhodesiana *occurs throughout the Eastern Highlands from Chimanimani to Nyanga at altitudes of over 1800m. As it is a plant of the open grasslands, the stems are often burnt black by fire. From these stems rise a rosette of dull green leaves with tiny white teeth along the edges. There are one to three flower stems per plant.*

Aloe inyangensis *grows mainly along the edge of the escarpment and other high exposed areas such as Rukotso, Mangua and Nyangani. The leaves arise from near the base of the stem and the plants form dense clumps. There are blooms at times throughout the summer months, although those at Mtarazi Falls start even as early as June.*

# Gloriosa superba

flame lily, jongwe

*This plant is tall and slender and climbs by clinging on to the surrounding vegetation with its curled leaf tips. The beautiful flowers have wavy-edged petals that curve upward and inward. All parts of the flame lily are very poisonous. It is a specially protected plant.*

## Lycopodium

clubmosses                                    LYCOPODIACEÆ

*This family is a relic of a very ancient fossil order of plants. The name comes from the Greek language and means 'wolf's foot'. These five species have all been collected in the Pungwe area.*

Lycopodium clavatum *is by far the most common. Whole hillsides are often covered by this plant which grows in the dappled shade of* Hypericum revolutum *or other shrubs.*

*When the spore capsules ripen, a cloud of yellow dust-like spores is released. This powder is highly inflammable and, in the past, was used by magicians to produce flashes of light.*

Both L. ophioglossoides *and* L. dacrydioides *are epiphytic although sometimes found on rocks in the deep shade of the Pungwe gorge. They hang downwards.*

L. carolinianum var. grandfolium *grows in soak areas, between tufts of grass out in the open, and is associated with* Sphagnum africanum *moss.*

Lycopodium cernuum *looks like little christmas trees, especially when the strobili (capsules) which hang down from the tips of the branches are ripe and a rich yellow. It is sometimes found growing on roadside banks.*

## *Erythrocephalum zambesianum*

red rays    (30cm)    ASTERACEÆ

*Grows in the musasa areas of Juliasdale and lower Troutbeck. The leaves are a silver green with a white felted undersurface which makes the deep scarlet of the flowers even more startling. The seeds germinate readily and the plant makes an attractive garden perennial as it is compact and well shaped. The generic name, erythrocephalum, means 'red head', which is appropriate.*

This group of plants was found growing in a soak area near the Pungwe River.

## Gerardiina angolensis

(30cm)   SCROPHULARIACEÆ

*Its leaves are held close to the stem.*

## Eriocaulon intrusum

(10cm)   ERIOCAULACEÆ

*The vivid green rosettes of the 'pipewort' bear many slender stems capped with little round heads of tiny flowers.*

## Utricularia prehensilis

(8cm)   LENTIBULARIACEÆ

*This little yellow snapdragon-like flower is an interesting plant as it has minute leaves. At the base of these leaves are tiny bladders that trap insects.*

## Ranunculus multifidus

(50cm)   RANUNCULACEÆ

*The yellow buttercup grows in soak areas or wherever there is wet soil. It flowers from October to January.*

These are both plants of the forest edge at altitudes below 1800m.

## Mussaenda arcuata

forest star    (3m)    RUBIACEÆ

A shrub with arching branches. The form of the flower is like a Japanese paper-sculpture, as the petals are folded down the middle and turned back. The star in the centre starts off a vivid orange and fades to a velvet brown.

## Harungana madagascariensis

orange-milk tree, mutseti    (5m)    CLUSIACEÆ

This tree has ochre velvet assegai-shaped leaves at the tip of every twig, which exude a bright orange sap if the leaves are pulled off, or a twig breaks. The sap is used for treating various ailments and as a dye.

## Strelitzia nicolai

giant strelitzia, mutsunde (8m)
STRELITZIACEÆ

*They are often found on rocky cliffs near waterfalls, including the Mtarazi and Pungwe falls.*

## Ensete ventricosum

wild banana, mutsoro (5m)
MUSACEÆ

*The wild banana, in spite of being cut down by frost every winter, grows alongside rivers and streams.*

## Dracaena steudneri

dragon tree, mukamba (8m)
DRACAENACEÆ

*The long green leaves are held in rosettes at the end of the slender stems.*

## *Angraecum chamaeanthus*

guava baby (actual size)  ORCHIDACEÆ

*There are also a number of epiphytic orchids in bloom. These range from the tiny guava baby, with leaves only 16mm long and flowers less than 2mm in diameter, to the giant* Bulbophyllum oxypterum *found growing on a tree in the forest below the Mtarazi Falls.*

## *Bulbophyllum scaberulum*

tree orchid, batanai  (30cm)  ORCHIDACEÆ

*The tree orchid illustrated below was found in the forest near the village of Buwu. The pseudobulbs are about 3cm long and well spaced along the rhizome which is often branched. The inflorescence is flattened like a blade and as it lengthens new flowers are produced. The flowers are a dull maroon and are in two rows on either side of the blade.*

*Sections of the rhizome between the pseudobulbs are used as splints when treating broken legs of animals in the Honde valley.*

# Zantedeschia albomaculata

subsp. *albomaculata*

yellow arum (50cm) ARACEÆ

The yellow arum lily with the deep maroon throat and erect leaves is fairly common throughout the area. The specific name means white-spotted, referring to the leaves, but more often than not, spots are absent. The leaves die down in winter and shoot again from the beginning of November.

The actual flowers are clustered around the spadix, and it is the yellow spathe that makes the show. Porcupines relish the roots and whole colonies of these arums may be uprooted during the night.

# Orchids

*The orchids shown here are of the open grasslands and able to survive fire by sheltering near rocks, or on the edge of wet ground.*

Brachycorythis pleistophylla *is a sturdy compact plant with tuberous roots. This specimen was 52cm tall, but they may be taller and are sometimes pink. (60cm)*

Disa aconitoides subsp. concinna *is a slender plant with mauve flowers with darker spots. It has a single conical spur. (60cm)*

Satyrium breve *has very short spurs. The flowers are a cochineal pink. It was found growing in a damp area, but in full sunlight. (50cm)*

# Bibliography and suggested reading

Ball, J. S.: *Southern African Epiphytic Orchids,* Conservation Press, Johannesburg, 1978.

Bassett, W. J.: 'A preliminary account of the vegetation and land use in the Inyanga Conservation Area', *Federal Department of Conservation (Salisbury) Technical Memorandum* 14, 1963.

Biegel, H. M. and Mavi, S.: *A Rhodesian Botanical Dictionary of African and English Plant Names* (2nd edition of the same title by H. Wild, 1953), Government Printer, Salisbury, 1972.

Burrows, J. E.: *Southern African Ferns and Fern Allies,* Frandsen Publishers, Sandton, 1990.

Coates Palgrave, K.: *Trees of Southern Africa*, C. Struik, Cape Town, 1983.

Drummond, R. B. and Coates Palgrave, K.: *Common Trees of the Highveld*, Longman Rhodesia, Salisbury, 1973.

Exell, A. W. and Wild, H. (editors): *Flora Zambesiaca*, Crown Agents for Oversea Governments and Administrations, London, 1960.

Guy, G. D.: 'Man and Plant at Inyanga', in *A Guide to the Antiquities of Inyanga* (metricated reprint of 1966 edition), Historical Monuments Commission, Bulawayo, 1972.

Heywood, V. H.: *Flowering Plants of the World*, Croom Helm, London, 1978.

Jacobsen, W. B. G.: *The Ferns and Fern Allies of Southern Africa,* Butterworths, Durban, 1983.

Kimberley, M. J.: *Excelsa* Nos. 1 & 2, Aloe, Cactus and Succulent Society of Rhodesia, Salisbury, 1972.

Levin, H., Granch, M., Rappoport, S. and Mitchell, D.: *A Field Guide to the Mushrooms of South Africa* (2nd edition), C. Struik, Cape Town, 1987.

Liggitt, B. and Fincham, R. J.: 'Gully erosion: the neglected dimension in soil research', *South African Journal of Science*, 85, (1), pp.18–20, 1989.

Lightfoot, C.: *Common Veld Grasses of Rhodesia* (2nd edition), Natural Resources Board of Rhodesia, Salisbury, 1975.

Martineau, R. A. S. and Phear, M. H.: *Rhodesian Wild Flowers*, Longmans, Green & Company, Cape Town, for the Trustees of the National Museums of Southern Rhodesia, 1953.

Onderstall, J.: *Transvaal Lowveld and Escarpment*, Botanical Society of South Africa, Cape Town, 1984.

Plowes, D. C. H. and Drummond, R. B.: *Wild Flowers of Zimbabwe* (2nd edition), Longman, Harare, 1991.

Schelpe, E. A.: *Flora Zambesiaca: Pteridophyta*, Crown Agents for Oversea Governments and Administrations, London, 1970.

Stewart, J., Linder, H. P., Schelpe, E. A. and Hall, A. V.: *Wild Orchids of Southern Africa*, Macmillan South Africa, Johannesburg, 1982.

Stocklmayer, V. R.: 'The geology of the country around Inyanga', *Rhodesia Geological Survey Bulletin* 79, 1978.

Summers, R.: *Inyanga – Prehistoric Settlements in Southern Rhodesia*, Cambridge University Press, Cambridge, for The Inyanga Research Fund, 1958.

Sutton, J. E. G.: 'Irrigation and soil-conservation in African agricultural history with a reconsideration of the Inyanga terracing (Zimbabwe) and Engaruka irrigation works (Tanzania)', *Journal of African History*, v. 25, pp. 25–41, 1984.

Sutton, J. E. G.: 'More on the cultivation terraces of Nyanga: the case for cattle-manure', *Zimbabwe Prehistory*, No. 20, pp. 21–24, 1988.

Tomlinson, R. W.: 'The Inyanga area – an essay in regional biogeography', *University of Rhodesia Series in Science: Occasional Paper 1*, Salisbury, 1973.

Tredgold, M. H. and Biegel, H. M.: *Rhodesian Wild Flowers*, Trustees of National Museums and Monuments of Rhodesia, 1979.

Tredgold, M. H.: *Food Plants of Zimbabwe*, Mambo Press, Gweru, 1986.

Tyndale-Biscoe, R.: 'The geology of a portion of the Inyanga district', *Southern Rhodesia Geological Survey Short Report* 37, 1957.

West, O.: *A Field Guide to the Aloes of Rhodesia*, Longman, Salisbury, 1974.

Wild, H.: 'Botanical notes relating to the Van Niekerk Ruins', in R. Summers *op. cit.*

Wild, H. and Fernandes, A. (editors): *Flora Zambesiaca* supplement: 'Vegetation map of the Flora Zambesiaca area', M. O. Collins, Salisbury, for the Governments of Portugal, Malawi, Zambia, Rhodesia and the United Kingdom, Salisbury, 1968.

# Index to family names and groups

ACANTHACEÆ *page*
*Thunbergia alata* 83
*Thunbergia lancifolia* 144

ALLIACEÆ
*Tulbaghia friesii* 136

ALOEACEÆ
*Aloe arborescens* 98
*Aloe cameronii* var. *bondana* 101
*Aloe greatheadii* 99
*Aloe inyangensis* 166
*Aloe maculata* 154
*Aloe myriacantha* 70
*Aloe pretoriensis* 107
*Aloe rhodesiana* 166
*Aloe swynnertonii* 99

AMARYLLIDACEÆ
*Boophane disticha* 148
*Crinum macowanii* 149
*Cyrtanthus contractus* 135
*Cyrtanthus rhodesianus* 135
*Scadoxus multiflorus* 71
*Scadoxus pole-evansii* 37

ANTHERICACEÆ
*Chlorophytum colubrinum* 31
*Chlorophytum galpinii* 156
*Chlorophytum* sp. 31
*Chlorophytum pygmaeum* 138

APIACEÆ
*Alepidea swynnertonii* 136
*Peucedanum nyassicum* 162
*Peucedanum rhodesicum* 162

ARACEÆ
*Zantedeschia albomaculata*
    subsp. *albomaculata* 175

ARALIACEÆ
*Cussonia spicata* 137

ASCLEPIADACEÆ
*Glossostelma carsonii* 25
*Huernia hislopii* subsp. *hislopii* 31
*Pachycarpus concolor* 147
*Trachycalymma fimbriatum* 147

ASPARAGACEÆ
*Myrsiphyllum asparagoides* 160
*Protasparagus africanus* 160
*Protasparagus plumosus* 160
*Protasparagus setaceus* 160
*Protasparagus virgatus* 160

ASPHODELACEÆ
*Kniphofia linearifolia* 44
*Kniphofia splendida* 44

ASTERACEÆ *page*
*Anisopappus kirkii* 74
*Athrixia rosmarinifolia* 129
*Berkheya zeyheri* 131
*Bidens formosa* 42
*Erythrocephalum zambesianum* 170
*Gazania krebsiana* subsp. *serrulata* 150
*Gnidia kraussiana* 131
*Haplocarpha thunbergii* 164
*Helichrysum adenocarpum* 79
*Helichrysum goetzeanum* 78
*Helichrysum herbaceum* 78
*Helichrysum nitens* 78
*Helichrysum nudifolium* 72
*Helichrysum odoratissimum* 72
*Helichrysum pilosellum* 131
*Helichrysum setosum* 78
*Helichrysum splendidum* 142
*Helichrysum sulphureo-fuscum* 78
*Helichrysum swynnertonii* 142
*Helichrysum umbraculigerum* 72
*Nidorella auriculata* 72
*Schistostephium artemisiifolium* 72
*Senecio deltoideus* 123
*Senecio latifolius* 131
*Senecio tamoides* 123
*Stoebe vulgaris* 139
*Vernonia calvoana*
    subsp. *meridionalis* 76
*Vernonia galpinii* 152
*Vernonia hirsuta* 136
*Vernonia karaguensis* 76
*Vernonia natalensis* 138

BALSAMINACEÆ
*Impatiens psychadelphoides* 58
*Impatiens sylvicola* 58

BASIDIOMYCETES (Fungi)
*Amanita muscaria* 50
*Boletus edulis* 50
*Clathrus archeri* 51
*Collybia* sp. 50
*Dictyophora indusiata* 50
*Macrolepiota zeyheri* 50
*Scleroderma cepa* 50
*Tremella* sp. 50

BEGONIACEÆ
*Begonia sonderiana* 59

BORAGINACEÆ
*Trichodesma physaloides* 127

BRACKET FUNGI
*Chondrostereum* sp. 114
*Coriolus versicolor* 114
*Fomes applanatus* 114
*Laschia thwaitesii* 114
*Pycnoporus sanguineus* 114
*Schizophyllum commune* 114
*Stereum hirsutum* 114

| BRYOPHYTES (mosses) | page |
| --- | --- |
| Introduction to mosses | 110 |
| *Campylopus procerus* | 111 |
| *Funaria spathulata* | 111 |
| *Leptodontium longicolle* | 111 |
| *Plagiochila divergens* | 111 |
| *Polytrichum commune* | 111 |
| *Rhodobryum* sp. | 111 |

| CAMPANULACEÆ | |
| --- | --- |
| *Wahlenbergia undulata* | 138 |

| CARYOPHYLLACEÆ | |
| --- | --- |
| *Silene burchellii* | 138 |

| CLUSIACEÆ | |
| --- | --- |
| *Harungana madagascariensis* | 172 |
| *Hypericum revolutum* | 117 |
| *Hypericum roeperianum* | 118 |

| COLCHICACEÆ | |
| --- | --- |
| *Androcymbium striatum* | 157 |
| *Gloriosa superba* | 167 |

| CONVOLVULACEÆ | |
| --- | --- |
| *Ipomoea involucrata* | 104 |

| CRASSULACEÆ | |
| --- | --- |
| *Crassula alticola* | 80 |
| *Crassula nodulosa* | 80 |
| *Crassula sarcocaulis* | 80 |
| *Crassula swaziensis* | 80 |
| *Crassula vaginata* | 80 |

| CUCURBITACEÆ | |
| --- | --- |
| *Momordica foetida* | 43 |

| CUPRESSACEÆ | |
| --- | --- |
| *Widdringtonia nodiflora* | 137 |

| CYPERACEÆ | |
| --- | --- |
| Mariscus hemisphaericus | 17 |

| DIPSACACEÆ | |
| --- | --- |
| *Scabiosa columbaria* | 152 |

| DRACAENACEÆ | |
| --- | --- |
| *Dracaena steudneri* | 173 |

| DROSERACEÆ | |
| --- | --- |
| *Drosera burkeana* | 67 |

| ERICACEÆ | |
| --- | --- |
| *Blaeria friesii* | 62 |
| *Erica johnstoniana* | 97 |
| *Erica simii ( = Philippia simii)* | 97 |
| *Erica whyteana* | 97 |

| ERIOCAULACEÆ | |
| --- | --- |
| *Eriocaulon intrusum* | 171 |

| ERIOSPERMACEÆ | |
| --- | --- |
| *Eriospermum cecilii* | 138 |

| EUPHORBIACEÆ | |
| --- | --- |
| *Acalypha caperonioides* | 156 |
| *Euphorbia citrina* | 140 |
| *Euphorbia depauperata* | 140 |

| FABACEÆ | page |
| --- | --- |
| *Acacia abyssinica* | 102 |
| *Acacia mearnsii* | 134 |
| *Brachystegia spiciformis* | 116 |
| *Crotalaria valida* | 161 |
| *Dolichos kilimandscharicus* | 130, 161 |
| *Erythrina latissima* | 153 |
| *Erythrina lysistemon* | 119 |
| *Indigofera hilaris* | 130 |
| *Lotus namulensis* | 130 |
| *Rhynchosia monophylla* | 130 |
| *Tephrosia grandibracteata* | 104 |
| *Vigna gazensis* | 104 |
| *Vigna macrorhyncha* | 161 |

| GENTIANACEÆ | |
| --- | --- |
| *Chironia gratissima* | 23 |
| *Sebaea longicaulis* | 64 |
| *Sebaea leiostyla* | 161 |
| *Swertia welwitschii* | 161 |

| GERANIACEÆ | |
| --- | --- |
| *Geranium nyassense* | 145 |
| *Pelargonium graveolens* | 145 |
| *Pelargonium luridum* | 145 |

| GESNERIACEÆ | |
| --- | --- |
| *Streptocarpus eylesii* | 47 |
| *Streptocarpus pumilus* | 47 |
| *Streptocarpus umtalensis* | |
| *(Nyangani* form) | 22 |

| HYACINTHACEÆ | |
| --- | --- |
| *Albuca kirkii* | 136 |
| *Eucomis autumnalis* | 36 |
| *Ledebouria revoluta* | 138 |
| *Ledebouria* sp. | 152 |
| *Scilla nervosa* | 152 |

| HYPOXIDACEÆ | |
| --- | --- |
| *Hypoxis angustifolia* | 146 |
| *Hypoxis obtusa* | 146 |
| *Hypoxis pungwensis* | 146 |

| IRIDACEÆ | |
| --- | --- |
| *Aristea ecklonii* | 159 |
| *Aristea woodii* | 159 |
| *Crocosmia aurea* | 41 |
| *Dierama formosum* | 159 |
| *Dierama inyangense* | 57 |
| *Gladiolus dalenii* | 38 |
| *Gladiolus gracillimus* | 45 |
| *Gladiolus masukuensis* | 45 |
| *Lapeirousia odoratissima* | 25 |
| *Moraea carsonii* | 41 |
| *Moraea spathulata* | 41 |
| *Radinosiphon leptostachya* | 25 |
| *Schizostylis coccinea* | 26 |

LAMIACEÆ page

Acrocephalus chirindensis 75
Aeolianthus buchnerianus 69
Aeolianthus rehmannii 31
Hemizygia teucriifolia 104, 129
Leonotis mollissima 74
Plectranthus hereroensis 69, 104
Plectranthus stenophyllus 161
Plectranthus zatarhendi 69
Salvia nilotica 161
Tetradenia riparia 104

LENTIBULARIACEÆ

Utricularia prehensilis 171

LICHENES

Lichens 112

LILIACEÆ

Lilium formosanum 42

LOBELIACEÆ

Lobelia erinus 133
Lobelia goetzei 133
Monopsis decipiens 133

LOGANIACEÆ

Buddleja auriculata 124
Buddleja salviifolia 104, 124

LUZURIAGACEÆ

Behnia reticulata 160

LYCOPODIACEÆ

Lycopodium carolinianum
var. grandifolium 168
Lycopodium cernuum 169
Lycopodium clavatum 168
Lycopodium dacrydioides 169
Lycopodium ophioglossoides 169

MALVACEÆ

Hibiscus meeusei 75
Pavonia columella 75

MELASTOMATACEÆ

Dissotis canescens 61
Dissotis princeps 100

MENISPERMACEÆ

Stephania abyssinica 83

MUSACEÆ

Ensete ventricosum 173

ORCHIDACEÆ

Aerangis mystacidii 65
Angraecopsis parviflora 63
Angraecum chamaeanthus 174
Brachycorythis pleistophylla 176

ORCHIDACEÆ (continued) page

Brownleea maculata 63
Brownleea parviflora 66
Bulbophyllum oxypterum 174
Bulbophyllum scaberulum 174
Cynorkis hanningtonii 29
Cynorkis kassneriana 52
Disa aconitoides subsp. concinna 176
Disa fragrans 66
Disa ochrostachya 49
Disa patula var. transvaalensis 49
Disa saxicola 35
Disa versicolor 28
Disperis anthoceros 52
Disperis virginalis 52
Eulophia nigricans 34
Eulophia odontoglossa 34
Eulophia streptopetala 151
Eulophia zeyheri 151
Habenaria clavata 29
Habenaria subaequalis 46
Herschelianthe baurii 132
Liparis bowkeri 53
Oberonia disticha 24
Polystachya concreta 63
Polystachya cultriformis 33
Polystachya hollandii 108
Polystachya ottoniana 32
Satyrium breve 176
Satyrium chlorocorys 40
Satyrium longicauda 28
Satyrium trinerve 27
Schizochilus cecilii 46
Stenoglottis fimbriata 53
Tridactyle bicaudata 63
Tridactyle tricuspis 68

PASSIFLORACEÆ

Basananthe sandersonii 138

PINACEÆ

Pinus patula 134

PIPERACEÆ

Piper capense 54

POACEÆ

Axonopus affinis 84
Cymbopogon nardus 84
Hyparrhenia filipendula 84
Isachne mauritiana 81
Loudetia simplex 84
Melinis minutiflora 84
Melinis repens 84
Monocymbium ceresiiforme 84
Panicum monticola 84
Themeda triandra 84

POLYGALACEÆ *page*
Polygala virgata 104

POLYGONACEÆ
Rumex sagittatus 83

PROTEACEÆ
Faurea saligna 103
Protea angolensis var. divaricata 96
Protea caffra 60

PTERIDOPHYTA (ferns)
Introduction to ferns 86
Arthropteris monocarpa 90
Arthropteris orientalis 94
Asplenium aethiopicum 89
Asplenium anisophyllum 88
Asplenium friesiorum 89
Asplenium hypomelas 88
Asplenium lobatum
    var. pseudoabyssinicum 88
Asplenium protensum 88
Asplenium sandersonii 88, 91
Asplenium rutifolium 88
Asplenium theciferum 88
Blechnum attenuatum 90
Cheilanthes multifida 92
Cyathea dregei 93, 126
Dryopteris inaequalis 87
Elaphoglossum aubertii 90
Gleichenia umbraculifera 92
Loxogramme lanceolata 87
Nephrolepis undulata 91
Pellaea calomelanos
    var. swynnertoniana 87
Pellaea doniana 94
Pleopeltis excavata 87
Pteridium aquilinum 128
Tectaria gemmifera 91
Thelypteris confluens 67
Vittaria isoetifolia 92

RANUNCULACEÆ
Clematis brachiata 77
Clematopsis villosa 30, 109
Knowltonia transvaalensis 128
Ranunculus multifidus 171

ROSACEÆ
Rubus rigidus 121

RUBIACEÆ *page*
Mussaenda arcuata 172
Otiophora inyangana 156
Pentanisia sykesii 129

SCROPHULARIACEÆ
Craterostigma lanceolatum 56
Craterostigma plantagineum 56
Cycnium adonense 129
Freylinia tropica 104
Gerardiina angolensis 171
Graderia scabra 129
Halleria lucida 122
Harveya randii 136
Hebenstretia oatesii
    subsp. inyangana 64
Lindernia pulchella 150
Selago thyrsoidea
    var. austrorhodesiaca 106
Sopubia mannii 48
Striga elegans 56
Sutera carvalhoi 109
Walafrida goetzei 106
Zaluzianskya sp. 56

SELAGINELLACEÆ
Selaginella abyssinica 81

SMILACACEÆ
Smilax anceps 121

STERCULIACEÆ
Dombeya burgessiae 75

STRELITZIACEÆ
Strelitzia nicolai 173

THYMELAEACEÆ
Passerina montana 163

TILIACEÆ
Sparrmannia ricinocarpa 74
Triumfetta welwitschii 143

VELLOZIACEÆ
Xerophyta equisetoides 158

VERBENACEÆ
Lantana sp. 74

VIOLACEÆ
Viola abyssinica 81

VITACEÆ
Cyphostemma montanum 83

# Index to plants illustrated and common names

Acacia abyssinica 102
Acacia mearnsii 134
Acalypha caperonioides 156
Acrocephalus chirindensis 75
Aeollanthus buchnerianus 69
Aeollanthus rehmannii 31
Aerangis mystacidii 65
african crocus 157
Albuca kirkii 136
Alepidea swynnertonii 136
Aloe arborescens 98
Aloe cameronii var. bondana 101
Aloe greatheadii 99
Aloe inyangensis 166
Aloe maculata 154
Aloe myriacantha 70
Aloe pretoriensis 107
Aloe rhodesiana 166
Aloe swynnertonii 99
Amanita muscaria 50
Androcymbium striatum 157
Angraecopsis parviflora 63
Angraecum chamaeanthus 174
Anisopappus kirkii 74
Aristea ecklonii 159
Aristea woodii 159
Arthropteris monocarpa 90
Arthropteris orientalis 94
Asplenium aethiopicum 89
Asplenium anisophyllum 88
Asplenium friesiorum 89
Asplenium hypomelas 88
Asplenium lobatum
    var. pseudoabyssinicum 88
Asplenium protensum 88
Asplenium rutifolium 88
Asplenium sandersonii 88, 91
Asplenium theciferum 88
Athrixia rosmarinifolia 129
Axonopus affinis 84

banana orchid 151
Basananthe sandersonii 138
beechwood 103
Begonia sonderiana 59
Behnia reticulata 160
bells of St. Mary's 127
Berkheya zeyheri 131
Bidens formosa 42
black-eyed susan 82
Blaeria friesii 62
Blechnum attenuatum 90
blue moraea 40
blue thunbergia 144
Boletus edulis 50
Boophane disticha 148
Brachycorythis pleistophylla 176
Brachystegia spiciformis 116
bracken 128
bramble 121
broad-leaved coral tree 153
Brownleea maculata 63
Brownleea parviflora 66
Buddleja auriculata 124
Buddleja salviifolia 104, 124
Bulbophyllum oxypterum 174
Bulbophyllum scaberulum 174
bush aloe 98
busy lizzies 58
buttercup 171
butterfly bush 124

cameron's aloe 101
Campylopus procerus 111

canary creeper 123
cape fig 16
Cheilanthes multifida 92
Chironia gratissima 23
Chlorophytum colubrinum 31
Chlorophytum galpinii 156
Chlorophytum pygmaeum 138
Chlorophytum sp. 31
chocolate bells 127
Chondrostereum sp. 114
Ciathrus archeri 51
Clematis brachiata 77
Clematopsis villosa 30, 109
climbing sorrel 83
clubmosses 168
Collybia sp. 50
Coriolus versicolor 114
cosmos 42
Crassula alticola 80
Crassula nodulosa 80
Crassula sarcocaulis 80
Crassula swaziensis 80
Crassula vaginata 80
Craterostigma lanceolatum 56
Craterostigma plantagineum 56
Crinum macowanii 149
Crocosmia aurea 41
Crotalaria valida 161
curry bush 117
Cussonia spicata 16, 17, 137
Cyathea dregei 93, 126
Cycnium adonense 129
Cymbopogon nardus 84
Cynorkis hanningtonii 29
Cynorkis kassneriana 52
Cyphostemma montanum 83
Cyrtanthus contractus 135
Cyrtanthus rhodesianus 135

Dictyophora indusiata 50
Dierama formosum 159
Dierama inyangense 57
Disa aconitoides subsp. concinna 176
Disa fragrans 66
Disa ochrostachya 49
Disa patula var. transvaalensis 49
Disa saxicola 35
Disa versicolor 28
Disperis anthoceros 52
Disperis virginalis 52
Dissotis canescens 61
Dissotis princeps 100
Dolichos kilimandscharicus 130, 161
Dombeya burgessiae 75
Dracaena steudneri 173
dragon tree 173
Drosera burkeana 67
drumsticks 56
Dryopteris inaequalis 87

eared buddleja 124
eastern district's lucky bean tree 119
Elaphoglossum aubertii 90
Ensete ventricosum 173
Erica johnstoniana 97
Erica simii (= Philippia simii) 97
Erica whyteana 97
Eriocaulon intrusum 171
Eriospermum cecilii 138
Erythrina latissima 153
Erythrina lysistemon 119
Erythrocephalum zambesianum 170
Eucomis autumnalis 36
Eulophia nigricans 34

Eulophia odontoglossa 34
Eulophia streptopetala 151
Eulophia zeyheri 151
Euphorbia citrina 140
Euphorbia depauperata 140

Faurea saligna 103
Ficus sur 16
Ficus thonningii 16
fire lily 135
fire pea 130
flame lily 167
florists' moss 111
fly agaric 50
Fomes applanatus 114
forest star 172
Freylinia tropica 104
Funaria spathulata 111

Gazania krebsiana subsp. serrulata 150
gazania 150
Geranium ryassense 145
geranium 145
Gerardiina angolensis 171
giant strelitzia 173
ginger bush 104
Gladiolus dalenii 38
Gladiolus gracillimus 45
Gladiolus masukuensis 45
Gleichenia umbraculifera 92
Gloriosa superba 167
Glossostelma carsonii 25
Gnidia kraussiana 131
golden candle orchid 49
Graderia scabra 129
grass aloe 70
guava baby 174

Habenaria clavata 29
Habenaria subaequalis 46
Halleria lucida 122
Haplocarpha thunbergii 164
Harungana madagascariensis 172
Harveya randii 136
Hebenstretia oatesii subsp. inyangana 64
Helichrysum adenocarpum 79
Helichrysum goetzeanum 78
Helichrysum herbaceum 78
Helichrysum nitens 78
Helichrysum nudifolium 72
Helichrysum odoratissimum 72
Helichrysum pilosellum 131
Helichrysum setosum 78
Helichrysum splendidum 142
Helichrysum sulphureo-fuscum 78
Helichrysum swynnertonii 142
Helichrysum umbraculigerum 72
Hemizygia teucriifolia 104, 129
Herschelianthe baurii 132
Hibiscus meeusei 75
Huernia hislopii subsp. hislopii 31
Hyparrhenia filipendula 84
Hypericum revolutum 117
Hypericum roeperianum 118
Hypoxis angustifolia 146
Hypoxis obtusa 146
Hypoxis pungwensis 146

Impatiens psychadelphoides 58
Impatiens sylvicola 58
Indigofera hilaris 130
ink plant 129
Ipomoea involucrata 104
Isachne mauritiana 81

*Juniperus procera* 15

*Kniphofia linearifolia* 44
*Kniphofia splendida* 44
*Knowltonia transvaalensis* 128

*Lantana* sp. 74
*Lapeirousia odoratissima* 25
*Laschia thwaitesii* 114
*Ledebouria revoluta* 138
*Ledebouria* sp. 152
*Leonotis mollissima* 74
*Leptodontium longicolle* 111
*Leucosidea sericea* 15, 16
Lichens 112
*Lilium formosanum* 42
*Lindernia pulchella* 150
lion's tail 74
*Liparis bowkeri* 53
little men in boats 157
*Lobelia erinus* 133
*Lobelia goetzei* 133
*Lotus namulensis* 130
*Loudetia simplex* 84
*Loxogramme lanceolata* 87
*Lycopodium carolinianum*
     var. *grandifolium* 168
*Lycopodium cernuum* 169
*Lycopodium clavatum* 168
*Lycopodium dacrydioides* 169
*Lycopodium ophioglossoides* 169

*Macrolepiota zeyheri* 50
manica daisy 129
*Mariscus hemisphaericus* 17
*Melinis minutiflora* 84
*Melinis repens* 84
milkweed 147
mole's spectacles 150
*Momordica foetida* 43
*Monocymbium ceresiiforme* 84
*Monopsis decipiens* 133
*Moraea carsonii* 41
*Moraea spathulata* 41
Moses in the basket 157
mountain cabbage tree 16, 137
mountain cedar 137
mountain sage 129
musasa 116
*Mussaenda arcuata* 172
*Myrsiphyllum asparagoides* 160

*Nephrolepis undulata* 91
*Nidorella auriculata* 72
northern protea 96
nyanga fire-ball 37
nyanga flat-top 102
nyanga hairbell 57
nyanga selago 106

*Oberonia disticha* 24
old man's beard 112
orange-milk tree 172
*Otiophora inyangana* 156

*Pachycarpus concolor* 147
*Panicum monticola* 84
parasol tree 14
*Passerina montana* 163
*Pavonia columella* 75
*Pelargonium graveolens* 145
*Pelargonium luridum* 145
*Pellaea calomelanos* var. *swynnertoniana* 87
*Pellaea doniana* 94
pencil-cedar 15

*Pentanisia sykesii* 129
*Peucedanum nyassicum* 162
*Peucedanum rhodesicum* 162
philippia 97
pineapple lily 36
pink everlasting 79
pink groundbells 129
pink heath 97
*Pinus patula* 134
*Piper capense* 54
pipewort 171
*Plagiochila divergens* 111
*Plectranthus hereroensis* 69, 104
*Plectranthus stenophyllus* 161
*Plectranthus zatarhendi* 69
*Pleopeltis excavata* 87
*Polygala virgata* 104
*Polyscias fulva* 14
*Polystachya concreta* 63
*Polystachya cultriformis* 33
*Polystachya hollandii* 108
*Polystachya ottoniana* 32
*Polytrichum commune* 111
*Protasparagus africanus* 160
*Protasparagus plumosus* 160
*Protasparagus setaceus* 160
*Protasparagus virgatus* 160
*Protea angolensis* var. *divaricata* 96
*Protea caffra* 60
*Pteridium aquilinum* 128
*Pycnoporus sanguineus* 114
pyjama flowers 157

*Radinosiphon leptostachya* 25
ragwort 131
*Ranunculus multifidus* 171
red rays 170
red stinkhorn 51
red-hot poker 44
*Rhodocryum* sp. 111
*Rhynchosia monophylla* 130
river lily 149
royal dissotis 100
*Rubus rigidus* 121
*Rumex sagittatus* 83

*Salvia nilotica* 161
*Satyrium breve* 176
*Satyrium chlorocorys* 40
*Satyrium longicauda* 28
*Satyrium trinerve* 27
*Scabiosa columbaria* 152
*Scadoxus multiflorus* 71
*Scadoxus pole-evansii* 37
scarlet river-lily 26
*Schistostephium artemisiifolius* 72
*Schizochilus cecilii* 46
*Schizophyllum commune* 114
*Schizostylis coccinea* 26
*Scilla nervosa* 152
*Scleroderma cepa* 50
scrambler 121, 123
*Sebaea leiostyla* 161
*Sebaea longicaulis* 64
*Selaginella abyssinica* 81
*Selago thyrsoidea* var. *austrorhodesiaca* 106
*Senecio deltoideus* 123
*Senecio latifolius* 131
*Senecio tamoides* 123
shock-headed peter 30, 109
*Silene burchellii* 138
*Smilax anceps* 121
*Sopubia mannii* 48
*Sparrmannia ricinocarpa* 74
spider lily 25

spotted leaf aloe 99
St. John's wort 118
star moss 111
*Stenoglottis fimbriata* 53
*Stephania abyssinica* 83
*Stereum hirsutum* 114
*Stoebe vulgaris* 139
*Strelitzia nicolai* 173
*Streptocarpus eylesii* 47
*Streptocarpus pumilus* 47
*Streptocarpus umtalensis* (Nyangani form) 22
*Striga elegans* 56
sun daisy 131
sundew 67
*Sutera carvalhoi* 109
*Swertia welwitschii* 161
sword fern 91
swynnerton's aloe 99

*Tectaria gemmifera* 91
*Tephrosia grandibracteata* 104
*Tetradenia riparia* 104
*Thelypteris confluens* 67
*Themeda triandra* 84
thick moss 111
*Thunbergia alata* 83
*Thunbergia lancifolia* 144
*Trachycalymma fimbriatum* 147
traveller's joy 77
tree fern 93, 126
tree fuchsia 122
tree orchid 174
*Tremella* sp. 50
*Trichodesma physaloides* 127
*Tridactyle bicaudata* 63
*Tridactyle tricuspis* 68
*Triumfetta welwitschii* 143
*Tulbaghia friesii* 136
tumbleweed 148

*Utricularia prehensilis* 171

vellozia 158
*Vernonia calvoana* subsp. *meridionalis* 76
*Vernonia galpinii* 152
*Vernonia hirsuta* 136
*Vernonia karaguensis* 76
*Vernonia natalensis* 138
*Vigna gazensis* 104
*Vigna macrorhyncha* 161
*Viola abyssinica* 81
*Vittaria isoetifolia* 92

*Wahlenbergia undulata* 138
*Walafrida goetzei* 106
white anenome 128
*Widdringtonia nodiflora* 137
wild banana 173
wild fig 16
wild garlic 136
wild lupin 130, 161
wild montbretia 40
wild pears 75
wild pepper 54
wild violet 81

*Xerophyta equisetoides* 158

yellow arum lily 175
yellow daisy 74, 164
yellow heads 131
yellow moraea 40
yellow stars 146

*Zaluzianskya* sp. 56
*Zantedeschia albomaculata*
     subsp. *albomaculata* 175